hang
tough
in a
hostile
WORLD

JOHN ALLAN LAVENDER

Based On
The Second Half of Hebrews

ACCENT BOOKS
Denver, Colorado

MEMBER OF
EVANGELICAL CHRISTIAN
PUBLISHERS ASSOCIATION

ACCENT BOOKS
A division of Accent-B/P Publications
12100 W. Sixth Avenue
P.O. Box 15337
Denver, Colorado 80215

Library of Congress Catalog Card Number: 77-93249

ISBN 0-916406-94-6

Contents

To
Margie Marshall
My gracious and gifted secretary who
does what the title of this book sug-
gests better than anyone I know.

How to Unlock the Treasure Chest

The following material appears as the introduction to *Hey! There's Hope!*, the companion to this volume. If you haven't yet read it, you may want to start there. However, each volume is designed to stand alone—to give you a sweet taste of the victory which God has prepared for you in this portion of scripture.

Hang Tough in a Hostile World will show you how your faith can grow stronger, regardless of how staggering the circumstances seem which confront you. And that's the treasure of the book of Hebrews: the joy you can find in the midst of sorrow. The peace, in spite of adversities. The "how to" of staying *up* when the world does its best to pull you *down*.

In Alexander Dumas' brilliant novel, *The Count of Monte Cristo,* a young man is wrongly accused of a crime and is imprisoned on a lonely, barren island.

In the dungeon he meets a monk who, sensing the character of the young man, tells him of a great treasure hidden on Monte Cristo, another island far away in a distant corner of the sea. Soon the monk dies.

Through a series of harrowing events, the young man escapes. He travels at great peril to the island where, following a map traced indelibly on his mind, he finds the hidden treasure. The monk, he discovers, had not exaggerated. There are gems and precious jewelry, objects of gold and silver in unbelievable abundance. Overnight, the youth is an extremely rich man.

In time, he becomes known as the Count of Monte Cristo. No one knows the source nor the extent of his wealth. He lives like a king with a never-ending supply of earthly riches. Whenever his bankroll gets low, he simply returns to the hidden treasure of Monte Cristo and replenishes his supply.

I propose that we follow the Count's practice in our approach to the book of Hebrews. Here, truly, is a treasure chest of spiritual riches in unimaginable abundance. Unfortunately for many of us, it remains *hidden* treasure. Apart from a few well-known passages, the typical Christian knows little or nothing of the vast wealth of hope and help God has tucked away in this virtually "deserted island."

As a beginning, therefore, let me take you to this treasure chest for a fresh look at the book of Hebrews, give you the key that unlocks it, and show you the riches God has put there. Then, like the Count of Monte Cristo, you can return at will and, chapter by chapter, take handfuls of these spiritual gems to provide resources for hopefull living.

Basically, there are two major interpretations of this most difficult book of the New Testament canon. Some expositors argue that the book of Hebrews was written to *Christians* who were in danger of falling from grace, thus losing their salvation. This is the classical Arminian view. A second group claims the book was addressed to mere *professing Christians,* those who had only come partway to Christ and were in danger of drawing back before being finally and actually converted. This is the position of most Calvinists.

Both of the above pose monumental problems, pitting one portion of scripture against another, in violation of solid Biblical scholarship. But there is *a third alternative,* one which appears to have been obscured or missed completely by most students of this treatise. This view solves the apparent mysteries surrounding certain seemingly contradictory texts, and I believe it does justice to the book of Hebrews, while remaining true to the total teaching of scripture.

It sees the book of Hebrews as having been addressed to born-again Christians. People who had been saved prior to the time the book was written, were still saved at the time this message was put into their hands, and would continue to be saved for all eternity. But—and here is the nitty-gritty of it—they were *sinner-saints*. Saved people who had allowed sin to gain a foothold in their lives, and who had lost the confidence derived from an intimate walk with Christ. Even worse, though they were born again, they were in grave peril of losing their future *reward*. Both the joys of an abundant walk with Christ here on earth and the benefits of such a walk in their life after death were on the line. Dealing creatively with the dual peril is the thrust of Hebrews.

THE TREASURE CHEST

Our first discovery is that there are a number of unanswered questions about this book. Who wrote it? When was it written? To whom was it addressed? Volumes have been written by scholars trying to unravel these mysteries, and we could speculate endlessly about them. But, when the Holy Spirit leaves certain questions unanswered, we should not be unduly distressed by His silence.

Our ability to appreciate and benefit from the treasure chest of Hebrews does not depend upon knowing as an absolute certainty who wrote it, what date it was written, or even to what specific place it was sent.

We *do* know this orphan book which begins like a sermon and ends like a letter was directed to a group of

Hebrew Christians who, under intense pressure from certain religious leaders and their Jewish friends, were in serious spiritual danger.

The author calls them "holy brethren, partakers of a heavenly calling" (Hebrews 3:1). He accuses them of being lazy and lethargic, on the verge of becoming spiritual dropouts. Through dull indifference they had lost much of their original dynamism. Their faith was stagnant. They had stopped growing spiritually. They had become lax in their church attendance, careless in their living and sloppy in their use of the scriptures. Their whole system of priorities was confused. They were no longer distinguishable from rank and file folk around them. Put simply, they were a lot like some of us!

We don't like to stand alone, either. We don't like to be isolated from our neighbors, family, or friends. The Hebrews' love of ease was no greater than ours. We, too, live by the myth that happiness is in having. So, when what we have is threatened, we are threatened. And, Christian or not, we tend to turn tail and duck for cover. Our "classification" drops from spiritual man (I Corinthians 2:15) to mere man (I Corinthians 3:4). We are saved sinners. Having no real reason for the hope that is within us, in the truest sense, we have no hope!

The solution is the same today as it was when the book of Hebrews was written: Jesus! God's answer then is God's answer now. Through this unknown penman, our heavenly Father urges all sinner-saints: Turn your eyes upon Jesus. Take a long, hard look at Him. Get with Him. Stay with Him. Go on with Him to real maturity.

This is the single theme running through this spiritual treasure chest. This is the one strong cord to which we are told to cling. Several strands intertwine to create this one sure cord of hope. They are graphically given in the outline which follows, "The Heart of Hebrews." As we carefully work our way through Hebrews, you will find these strands often so enmeshed with each other they are difficult to distinguish. For that reason, no attempt has been made to divide the book chapter by chapter, or verse by verse. The strands overlay each other. Weaving back and forth from first word to last. But they are there just the same.

LOOK AT ALL JESUS WAS! This is the first strand.

LOOK AT ALL JESUS DID! That's strand number two.

LOOK AT ALL JESUS MEANS! That's strand three.

This is the heart of Hebrews: *Jesus!* He is its richest treasure. Yet there are other precious jewels waiting to be discovered in this treasure chest. How do we unlock it to get to them?

THE KEY

I believe the key to this book is found in Hebrews itself, in verses 5:11—6:3. Here our author explains that there are many things that should but cannot be said because, sadly, these Christian believers never grew up!

"Concerning him we have much to say, and it is hard to explain, since you have become dull of hearing. For though by this time you ought to be teachers, you have need again for some one to teach you the elementary principles of the oracles of God, and you have come to need milk and not solid food. For every one who partakes only of milk is not accustomed to the word of righteousness, for he is a babe. But solid food is for the mature, who because of practice have their senses trained to discern good and evil. Therefore leaving the elementary teaching about the Christ, let us press on to maturity, not laying again a foundation of repentance from dead works and of faith toward God, of instruction about washings, and laying on of hands, and the resurrection of the dead, and

eternal judgment. And this we shall do, if God permits"
(5:11—6:3).

These seven verses form the key which unlocks the
treasure chest of Hebrews. They declare *the issue at stake
in Hebrews is not spiritual birth, but spiritual growth!*

The things said to these people in this particular
passage could not be said to non-Christians. Would the
Spirit of God say to a non-Christian, "You ought to be a
teacher of the word"? Would the Spirit of God say to a
non-Christian, "You ought to be eating meat," when
they couldn't digest milk? Would the Spirit of God say to
a non-Christian, "You should skip on past the fun-
damentals of repentance and faith in God"? The Spirit of
God would not insist people grow who had not yet been
born.

So, through this key passage, Hebrews interprets itself.
The people to whom this book refers were born-again
persons.

This is important. The Biblical references to the eternal
security of believers in Christ are numerous and clear.
They permit no uncertainty. "He who believes in the Son
has eternal life . . ."(John 3:36). "(Nothing) shall be
able to separate us from the love of God which is in
Christ Jesus our Lord" (Romans 8:39). ". . . No one is
able to snatch them out of the Father's hand" (John
10:29).

These and other references so frequently appear and
are so obvious as to be beyond debate. The Bible is God's
word and God does not contradict Himself. Therefore,
passages in the book of Hebrews which *seem* to suggest a
saved person can be lost again need to be examined closely. When seen in the light of this key passage (5:11—6:3),
we recognize that what is at stake is not *salvation*, but
reward.

In various portions of scripture, the Holy Spirit has

taken pains to warn it is possible to reject the lordship of Christ over our lives. It is possible right now to lose the joy of walking in company with Him. As a result, when we meet Him at the end of this life, it is possible that the reunion will not be all it should be. We will have nothing to present to Him if our works are burned by the fire of His judgment (I Corinthians 3:11-15). It is against that dreadful possibility that the writer of Hebrews hammers out the recurring theme: *GROW, CHRIST-IAN, GROW!*

One of our early Project Winsome Internationale lay leaders was an engineer named Dick Schoof. At a Leaders' Conference, Dick revealed that he had finally gotten that message.

"The more I know about the Christian life," he said, "the more I see it as a ladder leading to heaven. Being born again is mounting the first rung. From there on out, it's one rung after another. The further you go, the greater the distance between rungs. So, you'd better g-r-o-w!"

There's a lot of truth in that. And, it's in total harmony with what the book of Hebrews teaches: "For though by this time you ought to be teachers, you have need again for some one to teach you the elementary principles of the oracles of God, and you have come to need milk and not solid food" (5:12).

GROW, CHRIST-IAN, GROW! Grow intellectually! Move on from basic Christian teachings to the more demanding aspects of life. Speaking with the crisp candor of many Britons, Major Ian Thomas, a noted Bible scholar, once said to me:

"I'm sick and tired of hearing Christians tell me to preach the simple gospel. What they usually mean by this is, 'Tell me what I've always been told so I can hear what I've always heard. Then I can know what I've always

known, believe what I've always believed, sit like a cab-
bage in the pew and never think, never struggle, never
change, never grow.' ''

The prospect of thinking, struggling, changing and
growing is a painful one to many Jesus Folk. That's why
we must keep our heads on straight with a solid
knowledge of God's written word. These deep truths will
help immeasurably in our Christian growth.

Few writers have undertaken a practical approach to
the book of Hebrews. The reason for this must surely be
an abysmal ignorance on the part of many Christians,
coupled with a "Who cares anyway?" attitude about
such vagaries as the law, the prophets, the sacrificial
system and angels. Therefore, to say Christ is greater than
any of these means little or nothing to contemporary
Christians.

If you fit into that category, I hope this volume will in-
struct and help you understand the significance of these
things. This is a day when all God's children need a
reason to hope. If we're to have that reason and be able
to articulate that hope, we must grow up intellectually.
We must move on from the ABC's of theological
hairsplitting to something with teeth in it.

GROW, CHRIST-IAN! Grow spiritually! Maturity in
Christ means more than preoccupation with the elementary truths of Christianity—clutching a few theological
cliches. It means exchanging the typical for the actual.
Shadow for substance. Wrappings for reality. It means
putting meaning into verbiage we view as sacrosanct.

When Lucille and I became engaged, I presented her
with a large, exquisitely wrapped box. She could not contain her excitement. She took off the lovely wrappings,
opened the large box, and inside found a ring. Then do
you know what she did? She kept the wrappings and the
box and threw away the ring!

Of course not! Though the wrappings were beautiful, that beauty was completely diminished when she was face to face with the reality of the ring and what it symbolized. A complete change. A new life.

That's what the book of Hebrews is saying. You must begin a new life. But you must not stop there. You must undergo a complete change. Christian, you must stop fretting over whether you have been saying the right words. Or whether your baptism was as meaningful as it might have been. Or whether your understanding of communion is complete. Or whether you have all the "i's" dotted and the "t's" crossed in your theology about prophecy.

There are some things only faith can settle, as is so gloriously declared in Hebrews 11. If you have faith enough to believe God could bring the world into being out of nothing (11:3), you've got the faith for these first principles. These ABC's of Christianity. So accept them by faith, learn to hang tough in a hostile world, and go on to Christian maturity.

GROW, CHRIST-IAN, GROW! Grow personally. Go on from theory to practice. From creeds to deeds. Be willing to live for Christ now—regardless.

I don't know who said it, but it is said so well, "Faithfulness to doctrine is not mere faithfulness to beliefs, but to the whole of life. Obscure doctrine which delves into the past or future and makes its bed in picayune triviality is about as vital as studying the mating instincts of the gnat. Doctrine must have a bearing on life."

The message of Hebrews is *growth.* To go on from the so-called "simple gospel" to a "reason for the hope that is within you." As a saved sinner whom Satan tries to intimidate and neutralize by focusing attention on your many failures as a Christian, you must take a new look at

Jesus. Who He really was. What He really did. What He is continuing to do. Here on earth. *NOW*.

And, as your spiritual well runs dry from time to time, follow the practice of the Count of Monte Cristo: Return regularly to Hebrews, your "secret" source of spiritual treasure. Take much, so much that you cease to live in spiritual poverty, and experience spiritual abundance!

The Heart of Hebrews

I. LOOK AT ALL JESUS WAS!

A. **Greater than the Prophets**   1:1-3
(with their temporary, fragmentary message, for His message was final and complete)

B. **Greater than the Angels**   1:4-14
(who, at best, are only servants, while He is Son)

C. **Greater than Moses**   3:1-6
(to whom God gave the law, for Jesus is able to set men free from the law of sin and death)

D. **Greater than Joshua**   3:7—4:13
(who led the Israelites into an incomplete conquest, for Christ not only leads us in, but on to total victory)

E. **Greater than Aaron**   4:14—5:10
(the high priest, for Christ is the perfect priest who made the perfect sacrifice which need never be made again)

II. LOOK AT ALL JESUS DID!

A. Gave us a better Revelation   1:1-3
B. Gave us a better Relationship   1:4-14
C. Gave us a better HOPE   2:5—10:18
   1. What was meant to be will be!   2:5-18
     a. God's intention for man fulfilled in THE man   2:5-9
     b. A trailblazer for us by Christ   2:10-18
   2. Victorious life here and now   3:1-6
   3. Abundant life here and now   3:7—4:13
   4. Forgiveness and freedom

	here and now	4:14—10:18
a.	Through a better Covenant	8:1-6
	Providing better Promises	8:7-13
b.	Through a better Tabernacle	9:1-10, 23-24
	Equipped with a better Mediator	9:11-12
	Offering a better Sacrifice	9:23-28
	Achieving a better Result	10:1-18

III. LOOK AT ALL JESUS MEANS!

Because "we have" all that is declared above, "let us" avoid the ten deadly dangers of:

A.	Drift instead of Decision	2:1-4
B.	Hardened Hearts instead of Help in Time of Need	3:7—4:16
C.	Spiritual Infantilism instead of Christian Growth	5:11—6:3
D.	Laxity instead of Loyalty	6:4-20; 10:26-31; 12:15-17
E.	Wavering instead of Boldness	10:19-23
F.	Isolationism instead of Fellowship	10:24-25
G.	Weariness instead of Endurance	10:26-39
H.	Comfort instead of Discipline	12:1-11
I.	Dull Indifference instead of Grateful Response	12:25-29
J.	Expediency instead of Eternity	13:1-15

1

OUR HOPE: Jesus Helps Us Grow

Hebrews 6:4-12; 10:26-39

FOR in the case of those who have once been enlightened and have tasted of the heavenly gift and have been made partakers of the Holy Spirit, ⁵and have tasted the good word of God and the powers of the age to come, ⁶and then have fallen away, it is impossible to renew them again to repentance, since they again crucify to themselves the Son of God, and put Him to open shame. ⁷For ground that drinks the rain which often falls upon it and brings forth vegetation useful to those for whose sake it is also tilled, receives a blessing from God; ⁸but if it yields thorns and thistles, it is worthless and close to being cursed, and it ends up being burned. ⁹But, beloved, we are convinced of better things concerning you, and things that accompany salvation, though we are speaking in this way. ¹⁰For God is not unjust so as to forget your work and the love which you have shown toward His name, in having ministered and in still ministering to the saints. ¹¹And we desire that each one of you show the same diligence so as to realize the full assurance of hope until the end, ¹²that you may not be sluggish, but imitators of those who through faith and patience inherit the promises.

²⁶*For if we go on sinning willfully after receiving the knowledge of the truth, there no longer remains a sacrifice for sins,* ²⁷*but a certain terrifying expectation of judgment, and the fury of a fire which will consume the adversaries.* ²⁸*Anyone who has set aside the Law of Moses dies without mercy on the testimony of two or three witnesses.* ²⁹*How much severer punishment do you think he will deserve who has trampled under foot the Son of God, and has regarded as unclean the blood of the covenant by which he was sanctified, and has insulted the Spirit of grace?* ³⁰*For we know Him who said, "Vengeance is Mine, I will repay." And again, "The Lord will judge His people."* ³¹*It is a terrifying thing to fall into the hands of the living God.* ³²*But remember the former days, when, after being enlightened, you endured a great conflict of sufferings,* ³³*partly, by being made a public spectacle through reproaches and tribulations, and partly by becoming sharers with those who were so treated.* ³⁴*For you showed sympathy to the prisoners, and accepted joyfully the seizure of your property, knowing that you have for yourselves a better possession and an abiding one.* ³⁵*Therefore, do not throw away your confidence, which has a great reward.* ³⁶*For you have need of endurance, so that when you have done the will of God, you may receive what was promised.*

³⁷*For yet in a very little while,*
He who is coming will come, and will not delay.
³⁸*But My righteous one shall live by faith;*
And if he shrinks back, My soul has no pleasure in him.
³⁹*But we are not of those who shrink back to destruction, but of those who have faith to the preserving of the soul.*

A recent issue of *Reader's Digest* carried a story about a second-grader's exhibit in a primary school Science Fair. The exhibit consisted of a bright red flowerpot filled with rich-looking soil. Attached was the painful explanation in childish scrawl: *"Some seeds don't grow."*

There were several possible reasons for the lack of harvest. Too much water. Not enough sunshine. Inferior seed. Whatever the cause, there had been no growth.

In his comment on this poignantly humorous anecdote, Ian Chapman points out, "Unfortunately, many Christians must wear a similar sign on their person: *Some seeds don't grow!* And they haven't. Since their conversion experience, maturity has not come. The harvest has not been evident. Their experience with Christ is shallow and frothy."[1] Their lives have been a kind of spiritual dust bowl. Devoid of anything resembling growth.

The reasons for their spiritual sterility are as numerous as those which keep a seed from germinating, with one salient exception: There is nothing inferior about the Good News seed God plants in human hearts. The seed itself is flawless. The life force in it is strong. The potential for growth is eager for expression. So, if growth does not occur, we must look elsewhere for the cause.

That is precisely what the book of Hebrews urges and teaches us to do. The all-consuming practical concern of this book is what F. F. Bruce calls, "the grace of continuance."[2] Not, as some suggest, to preserve salvation, but in order that we who have been given the gift of new life might grow and produce a worthy harvest.

In chapter 10 of the companion to this volume, *Hey! There's Hope!*, we concluded that the peril described in Hebrews 6 and 10 is not hypothetical; that is, a kind of straw man put up to emphasize a point. Nor is it situational; for example, relating to first-century Hebrew Christians only. Nor people who were never really saved. Nor people who, once saved, were now lost. Rather, we concluded the peril described is actual. It constitutes a most serious danger to Christians who are accountable to God for their performance and productivity as Christians. But their present joy and future blessings are at stake, not their salvation.

The agricultural illustration (6:7,8) bears a strong similarity to Christ's parable of the sower (Matthew 13:24-30). It's almost as if this spokesman for questing Christians is preaching a sermon. Earlier, he had been talking about the supremacy of Jesus. Who He was. What He did. Now he pauses for a moment to make a present-day application, as if to say, "Do you remember the story which came down from our Lord Himself? The one about a man who went forth to sow, and how various kinds of ground produced various kinds of harvest? Well, let me give you a sequel to that parable. Land which produces is blessed by God. Land which does not produce is treated by God in such a way as to make it a blessing."

As he warms to his subject, we can almost hear him say, "The Master explained how the world is a vast composite of various kinds of soil. The seed is the Good News that life has come to the world. The Master implied that every man's life is a field of some sort. That every new birth is a planting. That the purpose of a planting is a crop. So our primary concern as Christians should be the harvest. That's the key issue. That's the matter of first importance.

"Now, I've been studying the harvest of some of your lives, and I don't like what I see. Let me warn you, therefore, of the dreadful danger you're in and show you what you can do about it."

Obviously, these are not the exact words of Hebrews. They are my paraphrase. But the message is the same. And it's the message we're concerned about.

What message is there for us today in Hebrews 6 and 10? Three thoughts leap out at me. First, the right kind of harvest is important. Second, the good farmer works hard to improve the soil to make a better harvest. Third, productivity never goes unnoticed or unrewarded.

THE RIGHT KIND OF HARVEST IS IMPORTANT

As a pastor, I can understand the appreciation and affection our author has for those within his sphere of concern who are living creative, positive, productive lives. He speaks of them in such endearing terms. "Beloved [my precious ones], we are convinced of better things concerning you, and things that accompany salvation . . . For God is not unjust so as to forget your work and the love which you have shown . . ." (6:9,10).

Thank God for Christians who produce a harvest under the most trying circumstances (10:32-34)! They are the joy, encouragement and temporal reward of the man who is privileged to be their pastor. Unfortunately, they are far too few.

Many Christians produce a pathetic crop. Their lives possess neither beauty nor usefulness when God needs them most. But to say such are not children of God would mean ruling out Noah, Abraham, Moses, David, Aaron, Solomon, Peter, John, Thomas, even Paul—each of whom, at various stages of his spiritual development, was unable to do the things he ought to do and to forsake the things he ought to forsake.

If sinful perfection were a prerequisite for salvation, no one would ever be saved! There is not enough merit in any of us. We cannot say believers who neglect their responsibilities and misappropriate God's blessings are not Christians. But we can say being a Christian and living like one are two different matters!

When someone claims to be a child of God but lives like the offspring of Satan, that person crucifies Jesus on his own account and holds Him up to contempt (6:6). That doesn't mean the person actually nails Jesus to the cross a second time. Rather, it describes the slow, steady, snuffing out of Christ's influence in his life as inwardly the person dies a little every day to the higher, nobler, sweeter, finer things of the Spirit.

Instead of doing as Paul did and crucifying the world (Galatians 6:14), egocentric sinner-saints crucify again the Son. Instead of letting Jesus be Lord of their lives, they insist on doing their own thing in their own way. Ego exerts itself. They permit self to usurp control. As a result, instead of Christ's life showing stronger and more clearly through that person, it grows weaker and more difficult to discern. Such Christians put Christ "to an open shame" (6:6, KJV).

There's an old saying to the effect that, for every person who reads the Bible, there are hundreds who read our lives. When we maintain our personal comfort by denying the Lordship of Christ over all of life, we deliver a body blow to Him and His body, the Church.

Someone asked Leslie Weatherhead what he had learned after forty years in the ministry. He said, "I have learned life will only work out one way and that's God's way." The famed preacher was right. Chip the corners off the cube of God's truth and invariably you lose. The world, the flesh and the devil use that jaded cube against you!

That's the whole point of this heavy emphasis on crucifying Christ in one's self and putting Him to shame. Jesus can stand the ridicule. He survived Peter's cursing denial and the other disciples' hurried abandonment. And, while it's true, as Dick Shephard observed, "The greatest handicap to the Church is the unsatisfactory lives of many Christians," the Church will survive.

But, when we crucify Jesus afresh, we kill something inside *ourselves*. And that's what the Father is concerned about. Not what sin does to Him, but what it does to His creation and the crown of that creation, you and me!

Part of the shame we bring to ourselves and the Lord Jesus through our rebel days and years is a harvest of bad fruit. It wouldn't be so bad if we only hurt ourselves. But there is a cycle of influence and reproduction we cannot escape. Bad fruit has a way of producing seed for more of the same.

Consider the irresponsible parents whose children grow up to be irresponsible parents. Witness the dope pusher who begets dope pushers. Think about the carnal Christian who, by his selfish example, pulls the spiritually newborn down to his level and produces another carnal Christian. Thus, since every man's life is a field and the New Birth is a planting, the pattern of growth and the quality of the crop should seriously concern us all.

THE GOOD FARMER WORKS HARD TO IMPROVE THE SOIL SO IT WILL PRODUCE A BETTER HARVEST

Ugly and unproductive ground is treated, sometimes harshly, in an effort to make it beautiful and useful. Depending on the condition in which the farmer first finds it, the process may be long and laborious. Or it may be relatively simple. But in every instance, the good farmer puts more into the ground than he takes out.

The improvement process may include leveling, grading, diking, irrigating and crop rotating, all aimed at enabling the ground to produce a better harvest. And, it's the farmer, not the farm, who is the best, most efficient judge of what is needed to improve the harvest. "For ground that drinks the rain which often falls upon it and brings forth vegetation useful to those for whose sake it is also tilled, receives a blessing from God" (6:7).

"The rain" speaks to me of that abundant grace of God which is lavishly given to all, despite their personal situation. The phrase, "useful to those for whose sake it is also tilled," points out that the purpose of land is not to serve itself, but to serve those who own it, till it, plant it, cultivate it. If the land is not fulfilling its intended purpose, the farmer has every right and obligation to treat the land in such a way as to enable it to do so.

Now, the point of all this is that God, the best of all husbandmen, is not indifferent to the factors which condition us and affect the quality of our soil as persons. In fact, because He gave us soul qualities of mind, emotion, and will, God accepts part of the responsibility for what we are and for doing something about it.

God is not an indifferent bystander. He is the wise and interested owner of the life-field of those who come to Him in Christ. ". . . You are not your own . . . you have been bought with a price . . ." (I Corinthians 6:19, 20). Having been "bought with a price," you belong to the buyer. God, the good farmer, is in the supreme position and knows what the soil of each Christian's life needs in order to produce a worthy harvest which will be useful to the One to whom the field belongs.

Our purpose as Christians is not to please and satisfy ourselves. Though that may seem unfair, it isn't. It's just another way of saying God's will for us is our highest good. God's will frees us from the frustrations, strain, and dissatisfaction of false productivity. It enables us to fulfill our intended purpose, which is where freedom and happiness lie. Freedom and happiness do not come from doing what we want to do, but from doing the things we were intended by God to do. Being the person we were intended to be.

A bird was made to fly. A fish to swim. Take them out of their element—expect the fish to fly or the bird to swim— and both lose their capacity to be happy and free. Similarly, the Christian was designed to grow and produce a harvest useful to God. If we are not fulfilling that purpose, because of sin or egocentricity, our heavenly husbandman uses all sorts of situations—some kind, some caustic—to help us become more productive and, thus, happier and freer. Happiness and freedom are by-products of accomplishing the things we were designed to do. Becoming the persons we were designed to be.

Sin and egocentricity always take a toll. There is no way you and I can get around that. The law of cause and effect always applies. In fact, there are only two courses we can follow when we err as sinner-saints. In both cases there are consequences. We can go God's way; which is to say, we can turn away from our sin and return to Him. When we do, the consequences of our sin remain in the form of psychic scars, lost blessings, irretrievable time and opportunity lost. But, by His grace, we do receive cleansing and forgiveness, plus an opportunity to start all over again, sadder but wiser.

Or, we can go our own way. We can persist in our rebellion and refuse to heed the gentle nudging of our God. If we choose this path, does the Lord smile benignly, shrug His shoulders and say, "Tsk, tsk"? No. Does He withdraw the gift of eternal life and send us to hell?

No. God neither ignores nor withdraws.

Then, what does happen when we start wrong and stay wrong? God, in His love, chastens us in the form of consequences which spring from our choices. "For this reason many among you are weak and sick, and a number sleep [have died]. But if we judged ourselves rightly, we should not be judged. But when we are judged, we are disciplined by the Lord in order that we may not be condemned along with the world" (I Corinthians 11:30-32).

Let me hasten to say, every sickness is not a sign of spiritual staleness. The Bible says rain falls on the just and the unjust as does the sunshine. (Matthew 5:45). The fact of our Christianity does not make us immune to illness. Nor does it surround us with a kind of invisible shield which protects us from catastrophe. All sickness and distress are not some form of chastening. God permits many things He does not will.

But the Bible and psychology both agree that unresolved guilt *can* make a person sick, weak and even lead to death. *Some* sickness, *some* weakness, *some* distress of spirit *are* consequences which God *permits* in order to prepare the soil of our lives for a better harvest.

God's disciplinary action is never an end in itself. It always has a purified person in mind as the ultimate result. The refiner's fire here on earth is aimed at removing the dross and producing pure gold which we may lay as a love gift at the feet of Jesus. A good farmer will go to almost any length to improve the soil so that it will produce a better harvest. God, the best of all husbandmen, is no exception.

No illustration is wholly apropos when trying to understand the ways of God. And this one, too, can be pushed too far. On the human level, the cost of treatment and development may be such that it is not economically feasible to save a certain piece of ground. But this is never true with God and His reconditioning of human soil. There are no lengths to which He will not go. No price He will not pay. The cross is evidence of that. And, following good farming practices in His treatment of human soil, God always puts in more than He takes out.

I shall never forget an automobile dealer in Kansas who said with joy and awe in his voice, "God is my partner. At the end of the year when my Partner and I add up the profits, He says, 'Bill, you take ninety percent and give me ten.' Wow! I'll do business with that kind of partner any day!"

This principle always applies: God gives more than He takes. But another principle also holds true: God will not force Himself on anyone.

The choice is ours. We can go God's way or we can go our own. In either case, there are consequences. Knowing this, how much better it is that we examine ourselves, judge ourselves, submit ourselves to the healing balm of God's forgiving grace. Which means we must not only confess our guilt. We must also commit ourselves to change.

Change is never easy. Our author is so conscious of the difficulty involved, he says, "It is impossible" (6:6). Note, please, that the apparent impossibility does not relate to renewing one to salvation, but to repentance. Also, there's no reference here to a limitation on God's grace. "For nothing will be impossible with God" (Luke 1:37).

An interesting characteristic of Hebrew literature is hyperbole; that is, deliberate exaggeration for emphasis. From the context, this word, "impossible," looks to me like an illustration of Hebrew hyperbole. In English, we may say about someone, "He or she is impossible!" By that we mean the person involved is extremely, even excruciatingly, difficult to deal with. I believe that's what the scripture is saying here. Practically speaking, it is "impossible," or psychologically improbable, certain carnal Christians will ever repent.

Many people have a penchant for tagging themselves as worthless. Hopeless. "Impossible." When they say this, it sounds like humility with a capital "H." Frankly, it's a first-class cop-out. To admit worth, hope and potential is to admit the possibility of change. But this puts the burden of action on one's own back. He becomes responsible for his attitudes and actions. Instead of wallowing around in the mire of self-pity, self-deprecation and self-deception, he must do something about himself. Change. Grow. Mature.

That's difficult. For some, it is practically "impossible." They are hardened saints. It is psychologically improbable they will ever respond, even to the amazing grace of God. But, what is psychologically true is not theologically true. With God, nothing is impossible. Anyone can change!

While one may not return to Him with the wonder and thrill of first-love repentance, it's entirely possible he will experience a different, deeper, dearer repentance. I've seen marriages restored which appeared to be hopelessly fractured because the love vow had been broken. When the offending partner handled the situation redemptively, a deeper, dearer love developed, binding the couple more closely to each other than before.

Even a Christian who openly and with cursing denies his Lord can be restored to fellowship and used in a wonderful way. Peter was! The same holds true for us. Does this mean we Jesus Folk should sin that grace may abound? God forbid (Romans 6:1,2). But when we do sin, if we permit God to deal with our sin and our self creatively, He will take that evil, transform it and, in a remarkable way, use it for His glory, our gladness and the world's good.

PRODUCTIVITY WILL NOT GO UNREWARDED OR UNNOTICED

"But, beloved, we are convinced of better things concerning you, and things that accompany salvation, though we are speaking in this way. For God is not unjust so as to forget your work and the love which you have shown toward His name, in having ministered and in still ministering to the saints. And we desire that each one of you show the same diligence so as to realize the full assurance of hope until the end, that you may not be sluggish, but imitators of those who through faith and patience inherit the promises" (6:9-12).

Our hope and joy as growing Christians come from two sources. They are the present and future products of trust and obedience on our part. They also derive from perfect memory on God's part.

Those of you who are growing are doing well, the writer of Hebrews says. Keep it up. The growing process will make your faith dynamic and alive. You will be able to move aside the mountains of life. You will get a kick out of being a Christian. The fact of your security in Christ will be supported by the feeling of assurance which comes from knowing all is well betweeen God and you.

Then, while you are trusting and obeying, remember God has a good memory. Human merit doesn't count. We only succeed in the Christian life by letting Christ live His life through us. Nevertheless, God is not unmindful of your sacrifice and your service of love. He knows what trust and obedience require. When He sees it, even though He has no obligation to do so, He rewards it well.

"Some seeds don't grow." Not because the seed is inferior, but because the soil is resistant. If you find this to

be true in the life-field of your own heart, remember God wants to work with you to improve your soil condition so you can produce a better, more satisfying harvest. Let Him. No, do more than that. Actively, eagerly, earnestly, wholeheartedly involve yourself with Him!

Ruth Calkin, the poet, put it in a loving and openly human way:

> When my rapport with You
> Is disturbed, Lord,
> My rapport with myself
> Is utterly destroyed.
>
> I am irritable
> Little things get in my way
> I am short with my family
> The house is too small
> My neighbors bore me
> The phone frustrates me
> Feelings of guilt gnaw at me.
>
> "Just leave me alone" I tell You,
> "I'll do it myself."
> But You patiently wait to be gracious,
> You gently nudge me to attention.
>
> For knowing me as You do,
> Loving me as You do,
> You understand so well
> That when I want You least
> I need You most.[3]

2

OUR HOPE: Jesus Jams Open the Door

Hebrews 6:13-20

FOR when God made the promise to Abraham, since He could swear by no one greater, He swore by Himself, [14]saying, "I will surely bless you, and I will surely multiply you." [15]And thus, having patiently waited, he obtained the promise. [16]For men swear by one greater than themselves, and with them an oath given as confirmation is an end of every dispute.

[17]In the same way God, desiring even more to show to the heirs of the promise the unchangeableness of His purpose, interposed with an oath, [18]in order that by two unchangeable things, in which it is impossible for God to lie, we may have strong encouragement, we who have fled for refuge in laying hold of the hope set before us.

[19]This hope we have as an anchor of the soul, a hope both sure and steadfast and one which enters within the veil, [20]where Jesus has entered as a forerunner for us, having become a high priest forever according to the order of Melchizedek.

If you were to try to isolate the primary area of your own personal spiritual concern, in all likelihood it could be reduced to two fundamental questions: *How do I get through to God? How do I know it when I've done it?*

These are primal questions. Central. Foundational. They have been from the beginning. Job, the oldest book in the Bible, raises the urgent question, "Where is God my Maker, Who gives songs in the night?" (35:10b). "Oh that I knew where I might find Him, that I might come to His seat!" (23:3).

The ancient Hebrews were harassed by the haunting questions of how one gained access to God and then knew it when it had happened. They were overwhelmed by a feeling of God's transcendence. His far-offness. His wholly other-ness. They were perennially plagued by the problem of bridging the awesome gap they conceived as existing between themselves and Jehovah. How could they gain access to Him? How could they do so with a sense of assurance that once in His presence they would be heard?

So, the central questions of your heart and mine are also those of these Hebrew Christians. We're all in the same boat. We want viable answers to our vital askings: How do I get through to God? How do I know it when I've done it?

Why is this so important? So crucial? So foundational? Because, if a person can really know he has access to God any moment of the night or day, and if he can feel assured that when he speaks God listens—that real communication occurs between them—any problem of any size can be solved. Or at least be handled creatively. With God's help, anything is possible. The key is getting through to God and knowing it.

It is this primal concern of the human heart to which the writer of Hebrews now directs our attention in a most interesting and intriguing way. Just prior to this (5:12—6:12), he has really been laying the leather to his listeners. You've been playing games with God, he says. You've been toying around with the Christian life. Nibbling at the edges of commitment. Going thus far, but no further. As a result, you've stopped growing. You've fooled with the spiritual ABC's so long, you've become spiritually DEF! God is speaking, but you won't listen. Or, worse yet, can't hear any more. Unless you snap to—repent—you're in for a rude awakening when you face Jesus at the judgment seat of Christ.

It's a severe rebuke. The warning is extremely solemn. Their spiritual indolence, indifference and immaturity are not laughing matters. These are not attitudes they can casually shrug off. But, being a man with a pastor's heart, the writer of Hebrews is not content to leave it there. Having shaken them to their roots with the severity of his exhortation, he suddenly shifts gears. He switches from bad news to good news. From rebuke to reassurance.

Shortly after I began my first pastorate, a prominent businessman met me at the door one Sunday, "Pastor, I like coming to this church and I may join it. I'm tired of being told *what* to do. I know that! The thing I appreciate is that, at long last, someone is trying to tell me *how* to do it."

Prior to his comment, I was not conscious of giving a

"how to" emphasis to my sermons. But following his comment, I made a deliberate effort to do so, because, as my friend pointed out, most of us know *what* to do. We're not stupid or morally insensitive. We know right from wrong. But knowing *how* to do it, and actually *doing* it, are where we need some help.

So, it's to the matter of teaching his readers how to grow in Christ that the writer of Hebrews now turns. "Do you want to grow in the Lord?" he seems to say. "Here's how to do it. You grow in the Lord by growing *in the Lord!* Like Abraham of old, you build your faith (and, consequently, your hope) upon the character of God Himself. You grow in the Lord by growing *in the Lord!*"

This reference to Abraham was especially effective, for those Hebrew Christians remembered that over the years God had made many promises to Abraham (Genesis 13:15; 15:5; 17:4-8; 22:17,18), and He had kept every one of them! (Notice that this man's name is spelled "Abram" in Genesis until God changed it in Genesis 17:5 to "Abraham," saying, ". . . for I will make you the father of a multitude of nations." At the same time God changed Sarai's name to Sarah, saying that she would bear a son and call his name Isaac (see verses 15-19).

Actually, these "extra" promises of God to Abraham were recapitulations, elaborations or clarifications, of His earlier promise to bless Abram and make him a great nation through whom the people of the world would bless themselves (Genesis 12:1-3). In fact, if there is an interpretive key which unlocks our understanding of the entire Biblical narrative, it is the covenant between God and Abram of Ur.

"Now the Lord said to Abram, 'Go forth from your country, and from your relatives and from you father's house, to the land which I will show you; and I will make you a great nation, and I will bless you, and make your name great; and so you shall be a blessing; and I will bless those who bless you, and the one who curses you I will curse. And in you all the families of the earth shall be blessed' '' (Genesis 12:1-3).

Abram was 75 years old and childless when God made this promise to him (Genesis 12:4). As the years rolled by, it became more and more unlikely that God could ever deliver on this particular commitment. As a matter of fact, Sarai, Abram's wife, made a joke out of the fact that a couple of senior citizens like them were one day going to have overflow crowds at their family reunions (Romans 4:18). But, as the decades went by and Sarai began to realize the seriousness with which Abram took God's promise, she decided to give the Lord a little help. She suggested her husband cohabit with Hagar, one of her maid-servants, and have a child by her.

I've often wondered why Abram succumbed to that particular suggestion. Because, while he was by no means perfect, he was a man of high principles. At one time, I thought it might have been that Hagar was a slick chick decked out in a B.C. version of the miniskirt who posed such an enticement the old boy couldn't handle it. However, when I recalled it was his wife who made this suggestion (knowing wives and the kind of women they'd pick for such an arrangement), I decided *Hag*ar was probably well named! I don't think Sarai was taking any chances!

But, whatever the reason, Abram took the bad advice of his misguided wife. Hagar conceived and bore Ishmael, who has proved to be a thorn in the side of Israel from that day to this. Finally, twenty-five years after God made His promise to Abram, Sarai conceived and Isaac, the child of promise, was born (Genesis 21:1-3).

As Abram watched this long-awaited son grow into

young manhood, he must have scratched his head at times and wondered if God had gotten His wires crossed. Ishmael was so aggressive, while Isaac was hardly the strongest character about which we read in scripture. He was constantly being manipulated. First, by his mother. Later by his wife. Yet, despite these Caspar Milquetoast qualities, Isaac was the child of promise. On him rested the fulfillment of God's prophecy regarding a great nation through whom the people of the world would bless themselves.

Therefore, the directions God gave to Abraham must have seemed absolutely incredible. ". . . God tested Abraham, and said to him . . . 'Take now your son, your only son, whom you love, Isaac, and go to the land of Moriah; and offer him there as a burnt offering on one of the mountains of which I will tell you' " (Genesis 22:1,2).

When, in complete trust and obedience, Abraham did as he was told, God intervened at the very last moment, a sacrificial ram was provided, Isacc was spared, and the burnt sacrifice proceeded on schedule. At this point, God restated His earlier promise to Abraham, confirming it with a remarkable oath. " '. . . By Myself I have sworn,' declares the Lord, 'because you have done this thing, and have not withheld your son, your only son, indeed I will greatly bless you, and I will greatly multiply your seed as the stars of the heavens, and as the sand which is on the seashore; and your seed shall possess the gate of their enemies. And in your seed all the nations of the earth shall be blessed, because you have obeyed My voice' " (Genesis 22:16-18).

Now, returning to Hebrews (6:13-20), we will see how this all comes together. To get the full picture, we must take into account the earnestness and seriousness with which an oath was held in those days. The easy perjury of our own day was almost unheard of in Biblical times.

An oath was the strongest surety a man could give. Usually, he invoked "the higher power" as a witness. If there were any question about the intentions of a person, the moment he swore in the name of the living God, saying such and such were so, that ended it. All speculation about his veracity was over. All doubts and misgivings were laid aside. The issue was settled. The deal was a deal.

With that background in mind, you can imagine the wide-eyed wonder of those who later read of this oath with which God had sealed His promise to Abraham. You can also begin to grasp why it was that they believed with unquestioning certainty that the prophecy regarding Abraham and his seed would be fulfilled.

Actually, of course, the mere fact that God said He would bless Abraham should have been enough. And it really was. His word is His bond. On the human level, though, that isn't always true; consequently, we sometimes have difficulty just accepting and believing God's word.

A number of years ago we had an opportunity to acquire a small cabin on a lovely lake in northern Wisconsin. The seller wanted cash and I was $5,000 short of being able to give it to him. While praying and thinking about what I might do, I was led to call a man in Chicago who had loaned money to churches on various occasions. I explained my problem to him, offering a first mortgage as collateral if he would loan me $5,000. He said he would think about it and call me back in a day or two.

A couple of days later when the phone rang, it was my friend, Van Maxson. "John, I've thought a great deal about this matter. You really should have that property. You work hard and take very little time off. You need a quiet place to get away so that the healing force of nature can do its work. But," he went on, "I've got more first mortgages now than I need. I don't want any more.

However, if you'll give me your word, I'll loan you the $5,000 without collateral!''

Obviously, I was overjoyed. Even more, I was deeply moved by this expression of trust. Later, he accepted a signed note for the benefit of his heirs, were he to die, but no reference was ever made to it. Now, do you think I would renege on that obligation? Never in a million years! I would have sold everything I owned and, if necessary, lived in a tent before I would have failed the kind of trust Van Maxson placed in me.

The comparison is hardly the same, but the point is, God's bare word should have been enough. And, from Abraham's point of view, I think it was. But maybe, remembering the earlier debacle involving Hagar and Ishmael, God decided to shore up Abraham on his weak side. Whatever the reason, on His own initiative, God confirmed His prior promise with an oath!

". . . He could swear by no one greater . . .'' (Hebrews 6:13), so He swore by *Himself*, making His covenant with Abraham doubly secure. God's word backed by God's good name! Two immutable—unchangeable, absolutely certain—things. Thus, the issue was settled. The prophecy was dependable. Abraham and his seed were indeed blessed to be a blessing.

For twenty-five years, God's word and God's oath were all Abraham had. A quarter of a century passed before Sarah conceived and bore Isaac. Yet, through all this time, the patriarch remained faithful. Why? Because he knew in his heart God could not be untrue to Himself.

That was exactly the point the writer of Hebrews wanted to make. You grow in the Lord by growing *in* the *Lord!* You must put your faith in *Him.* In *His* person. *His* promises. *His* power. Not in any quality or cleverness of your own.

God had promised to do something tremendous

through Abraham. "What God promised to do did not depend upon Abraham's worth, merit, works or conduct," says M. R. DeHaan,[1] "but upon God's person, God's promise and God's power to keep that promise. Biblical faith always rests in God. Never in itself or in the one who possesses it."

So, we Christians can be hopeful. Not because of our steadfastness. Our faithfulness. Our cleverness. Our courage. These are not the guarantee of our faith. We are hopeful because behind, in and through it all is the nature and character of God Himself. God, who makes promises and keeps them. "That's the kind of faith I want you to have," the writer of Hebrews says. Faith that rests in God.

Think about Abraham again. He didn't have faith because he saw immediate results. He had to wait two and a half decades before his son was born. He didn't have faith because it made sense. It was nonsense, unreasonable, to believe a couple of old codgers like Abraham and Sarah would conceive a child (Romans 4). Nor, was Abraham's faith strong because it was supported by the people around him. His own wife temporarily undermined his faith by giving him some bad advice.

The thing which made Abraham's faith effective, which kept hope alive, was its rootage in the nature of God Himself. Without seeing any result for twenty-five years, he clung to the character of God. That's what true faith always does. That's where true faith always rests.

Jane Merchant, a tremendous woman, is the victim of a baffling bone disease and has never walked. She was confined to a wheelchair at the age of two, and to her bed at the age of twelve. She lost her sight at the age of twenty-three, and now her hearing is gone. But in her darkness and despair, Jane Merchant found God. She reached out to Him. Believed what He said about Himself. Took a tremendous leap of faith, and, in the process, found hope.

She began writing poetry. Many of her poems have been printed in *McCalls, Harper's Bazaar, Good Housekeeping, Atlantic Monthly* and other magazines. One of her poems describes her pilgrimage:

> Full half a hundred times I've sobbed, "I can't go on";
> Yet, full half a hundred times I've hushed my sobs and gone.
> My answer if you ask me how, may seem presumptuously odd,
> But what keeps me keeping on when I cannot, is God.[2]

That's the answer to our quest for reality and certainty. God! The loving, gracious, giving, dependable nature of God. The man of faith does not praise his unconquerable soul. He praises God. He does not say, "What a good boy am I," but, "How great *Thou* art!" He does not say, "Seeing is believing," because he knows believing is seeing. Biblical faith always walks without benefit of sight, resting its case upon the nature of God. His fidelity. His justice. His mercy.

If you want to grow in the Lord, grow *in* the *Lord*. Get to know the truth about Him. Build your hope upon Him. Like Abraham, take Him at His word when it seems ridiculous to do so. And, like Abraham, you, too, shall see God work in mysterious ways His wonders to perform.

In college, my agnostic friends used to ask what they thought was a sophisticated question: Can God close and open a door at the same time? If you said no, you were admitting God was not omnipotent. The answer, of course, was, "Yes, He can, but He won't because God doesn't do stupid things!" God operates within laws He Himself has established because He knows keeping those laws is the highest good. When God makes a promise, He keeps it. Not because He has to, but because He chooses to. That's the way He is. That's His nature.

But, more often than not, there is a time lag between promise and performance. In Abram's case it was twenty-five years. During this time, between promise and performance, we have an opportunity to exercise our faith and, thus, make it stronger. When we fail to do that—when, despite what we say to the contrary, we act as if God were dead, or a weakling who cannot deliver on His promises—we miss the joy of proving Him good to His word, thus adding to our confidence. Fortifying our faith. Strengthening our hope. And that's a shame. We miss the blessings which could be ours if we would trust God while we still face our problems, rather than after the problem is solved.

What is the big hurdle facing you at the moment? What is the overriding problem confronting you right now? What is the area of supreme improbability in your life? Make it a matter of surrender to God. Now. Today. While the concern exists. Take one of God's promises and stand on it. The Bible is full of them. Then, like Abraham of old, let the good Lord work it out.

Remember the time lag, and use it as a time of testing. A time to walk by faith, not by sight. Be a bulldog of tenacious trust. Grab hold of the God who promises and refuses to let go. It may be a while before the answer comes. But when it comes, it will be doubly sweet. You and your faith will be better, stronger, more hopeful.

Perhaps you are thinking, "John, I'd like to do that. I'd like to cast myself in utter abandonment upon God.

But I've got that hang-up you wrote about earlier. I suffer from the dual anxiety of wondering: How do I get through to God and how do I know it when I've done it? Frankly, I don't see any connection between God's oath to Abraham and my own personal quest for reality and certainty."

Well, the relevance lies in the fact that the promise was to Abraham *and his seed* (Genesis 22:15-18). The Bible explains that Abraham's seed is not literal, but spiritual. "There is neither Jew nor Greek, there is neither slave nor free man, there is neither male nor female; for you are all one in Christ Jesus. And if you belong to Christ, then you are Abraham's offspring, heirs according to promise" (Galatians 3:28, 29).

The promise God first made to Abram of Ur has been extended to Christ's church. How do we know? Think about it. The covenant God made with Abram included two prophecies. First, his seed would be multiplied. Abraham lived to see that part of the prophecy fulfilled through the birth of his son and his grandsons. Second, through his seed, the nations of the world would be blessed. This phase of the prophecy only began to become true at the birth of Jesus, Israel's greatest son.

Now, if you have given yourself to Jesus Christ, been born again through Him, become part of His church through whom the world will be blessed and, at this very moment, is being brought back to God, then you are the spiritual seed of Abraham. Along with every other true believer, you are heir to all the promises God made to Abraham's seed in perpetuity.

This is the foundation stone upon which your faith rests. Heir to all the promises God made to Abraham. It is another wonderful reason for the hope which is within you as a Christian. Because God is God and His promises are doubly secure, you can get through to Him! And, you can know it when you've done it!

"In order that by two unchangeable things, in which it is impossible for God to lie, we may have strong encouragement, we who have fled for refuge in laying hold of the hope set before us. This hope we have as an anchor of the soul, a hope both sure and steadfast and one which enters within the veil, where Jesus has entered as a forerunner for us . . ." (Hebrews 6:18-20).

In chapters 4 and 5 we will look at the Old Testament tabernacle. We will see it as a magnificent foreshadowing of the ministry of Christ. We will study the outer court, the inner court, the various furnishings and the Holy of Holies which was behind the veil. It was there, in that holiest of places, God was felt to dwell. So sacred was this spot, only one person was permitted entry. The high priest. And then only once a year for a very short time. We shall see, in thrilling detail, how Christ, the perfect sacrifice, made the ancient annual sacrifice completely unnecessary, for He ministers in the true tabernacle of God, constantly making intercession on our behalf.

For the moment, however, I want you to see a wonderful truth. Here is something to savor. To revel in and wonder at. Here is another reason for the hope that is within you. Jesus has gone through, or beyond, the veil. By so doing, He has opened the way to God, not just for Himself, but for us—on our behalf (6:19).

God, who before Christ was thought to be a distant stranger, is now known to be a loving friend. Because Jesus has gone "within the veil," He who said, "I am the door" (John 10:9), has jammed the door open. And we, you and I, have access to God any time of the day or night. We have a place of refuge near to the heart of God. An anchor safe and sure (6:19). We have access to God and the assurance of being heard.

These references to a place of refuge (6:18) and an anchor safe and sure (6:19) are beautiful. The book of Numbers reveals a very interesting Old Testament provision (Numbers 35:9 ff). If a person accidentally killed someone and there were those who wanted to hold him accountable, possibly even put him to death, he could flee to what was called a "city of refuge." In that city, he was safe. He could not be unjustly punished (Deuteronomy 4:41-43; 19:5; Joshua 20).

Do you see it? God, in His loving grace has prepared a perfect place of refuge for those of us who are often in the role of fugitives. If we will flee to Jesus, we shall find Him to be our high and holy fortress, a strong shoulder on which to rest, a precious and loving Saviour in Whose company is fellowship and joy!

But, not only do we have a refuge, we have an anchor safe and sure. An anchor that rests, not in the hold of the ship, for our confidence is not in ourselves. Nor does it rest in shifting sands where it can be pulled loose by treacherous waves, for our confidence is not in our feelings which are affected by every wind of circumstance which blows. Rather, our anchor is "within the veil" (6:19). It is hooked on the "Rock of Ages." It is moored on the only real immovable object there is: the throne of God Himself. Thus, we are secure for time and eternity.

Amid all the storms of life, our anchor holds. It finds its certainty in God. In the fact that Jesus, who entered "within the veil," has opened the way to heaven and keeps it open. This is our hope. Jesus jams open the door. Therefore, we have access to God any time of the day or night. We can get through to Him. And, we can know it when we've done it!

3

OUR HOPE: Jesus – a Priest Like Mel Who?

Hebrews 7

FOR this Melchizedek, king of Salem, priest of the Most High God, who met Abraham as he was returning from the slaughter of the kings and blessed him, ²to whom also Abraham apportioned a tenth part of all the spoils, was first of all, by the translation of his name, king of righteousness, and then also king of Salem, which is king of peace. ³Without father, without mother, without genealogy, having neither beginning of days nor end of life, but made like the Son of God, he abides a priest perpetually.

⁴Now observe how great this man was to whom Abraham, the patriarch, gave a tenth of the choicest spoils. ⁵And those indeed of the sons of Levi who receive the priest's office have commandment in the Law to collect a tenth from the people, that is, from their brethren, although these are descended from Abraham.

⁶But the one whose genealogy is not traced from them collected a tenth from Abraham, and blessed the one who had the promises. ⁷But without any dispute the lesser is blessed by the greater. ⁸And in this case mortal men receive tithes, but in that

case one receives them, of whom it is witnessed that he lives on. ⁹And, so to speak, through Abraham even Levi, who received tithes, paid tithes, ¹⁰for he was still in the loins of his father when Melchizedek met him.

¹¹Now if perfection was through the Levitical priesthood (for on the basis of it the people received the Law), what further need was there for another priest to arise according to the order of Melchizedek, and not be designated according to the order of Aaron? ¹²For when the priesthood is changed, of necessity there takes place a change of law also. ¹³For the one concerning whom these things are spoken belongs to another tribe, from which no one has officiated at the altar. ¹⁴For it is evident that our Lord was descended from Judah, a tribe with reference to which Moses spoke nothing concerning priests.

¹⁵And this is clearer still, if another priest arises according to the likeness of Melchizedek, ¹⁶who has become such not on the basis of a law of physical requirement, but according to the power of an indestructible life. ¹⁷For it is witnessed of Him,

"Thou art a priest forever
According to the order of Melchizedek."

¹⁸For, on the one hand, there is a setting aside of a former commandment because of its weakness and uselessness ¹⁹(for the Law made nothing perfect), and on the other hand there is a bringing in of a better hope, through which we draw near to God.

²⁰And inasmuch as it was not without an oath ²¹(for they indeed became priests without an oath, but He with an oath through the One who said to Him,

"The Lord has sworn
And will not change His mind,

'Thou art a priest forever' ");
[22]*so much the more also Jesus has become the guarantee of a better covenant.* [23]*And the former priests, on the one hand, existed in greater numbers, because they were prevented by death from continuing,* [24]*but He, on the other hand, because He abides forever, holds His priesthood permanently.* [25]*Hence also He is able to save forever those who draw near to God through Him, since He always lives to make intercession for them.*

[26]*For it was fitting that we should have such a high priest, holy, innocent, undefiled, separated from sinners and exalted above the heavens;* [27]*who does not need daily, like those high priests, to offer up sacrifices, first for His own sins, and then for the sins of the people, because this He did once for all when He offered up Himself.* [28]*For the Law appoints men as high priests who are weak, but the word of the oath, which came after the Law, appoints a Son, made perfect forever.*

God's purpose in sending His Son into the world was not solely to make saints out of sinners, but having accomplished that, to make servants out of saints. Once we have become Christians, our primary purpose for being here is to be to the world what Christ would be if He were physically here Himself.

An attorney who properly understood his role and responsibility as a Christian was flying home from a legal convention. The only unoccupied seat on board was beside a young lady. They were barely airborne when he found a natural way to share his faith and to confront her with the person of Jesus Christ. It was a short flight. As he gathered his luggage at the baggage claim area, he met the young woman again, with her husband who had come to meet her. They exchanged pleasantries for a moment, said goodbye and parted.

As the lawyer left, her husband said, "Who was that guy?"

"Oh," she explained, "just a man I met on the airplane. And guess what?" she continued. "He asked me if I was a Christian."

"Did you tell him to mind his own business?" her husband asked.

She replied softly, "You know, dear, it sounds strange, but the way he talked it *was* his business."[1]

The young lady perceived an important truth. When a person is genuinely born again, it is pointless to tell him to mind his own business. He is no longer in business for himself. From salvation on, like his Lord, he must be about his Father's business. That involves being to the small sphere of his world what Christ would be if he were physically here Himself.

To equip us for this remarkable mission, the Holy Spirit has gone to great lengths to explain Who it is we represent. What His credentials are. How He is prepared to help us do our job. And, as usual, the author of Hebrews presents this necessary and supportive information in a most ingenious way.

To the modern mind, this reference to Melchizedek may not only seem mysterious, but actually superfluous. Some folk couldn't care less about Melchizedek. However, the book of Hebrews was written to give saved sinners a reason to hope. It does so by declaring who Jesus was. What Jesus did. How Jesus affects life today and in eternity. Thus, there is more here than meets the eye. Beneath the surface are great and abiding truths placed here by the Holy Spirit for our enlightenment and encouragement.

The writer of Hebrews has already explained that the priesthood of Melchizedek is something about which he will have "much to say" and that it will be "hard to explain" (5:11). Therefore, we are not surprised to find chapter 7 both fascinating and difficult. It contains some of the "solid food" maturing Christians should be eating (5:12).

Few figures in scripture are more mysterious than Melchizedek. He appears briefly in the Biblical narrative and then nothing more is heard of him. Like Topsy who just grew, Melchizedek is suddenly flung on the stage of history without hint of ancestry. Genesis 14 (verse 18) introduces him. Psalm 110 (verse 4) makes a brief prophetic statement about him. Add to these references the passages in Hebrews, and that's all we know about him.

Because of the mystery surrounding Melchizedek, there has been a great deal of speculation about who he was. Some have said he was a Christophany; that is, a visible, physical, pre-Bethlehem appearance of Jesus Himself. Others say he was some sort of supernatural messenger, maybe a mighty angel. The Jewish Torah identifies him as Shem, the son of Noah.

For my part, except to say by his actions and attitude he was an excellent prototype of Christ, I don't think it's necessary to get terribly exercised over the man. As Harry Ironside, the famed former pastor of Moody Church, once said, "If anyone asks 'Who is Melchizedek?' the only proper answer is: 'Melchizedek!' "[2]

Why, then, is he introduced at all? Genesis 14 provides a clue. Here is the story of a confederacy of kings which attacked Sodom and its sister cities. These kings succeeded in capturing the city-states, carried off a tremendous amount of loot and a large number of captives, including Lot, Abram's nephew. When Abram learned of Lot's disaster, he organized a small army of 318 well-trained, well-equipped servant-soldiers and set out in hot pursuit of the invaders. He overtook them near Damascus. Under cover of dark, using not-so-new guerrilla tactics, he launched a surprise attack. Routed the enemy. Recovered the captives and booty.

Word of his successful incursion apparently got back to the defeated king of Sodom. He went out to greet Abram (Genesis 14:17), to tell him he could retain the plunder he had recaptured from the confederacy of kings. However, before they met and the king of Sodom could make this tempting offer, Abram passed the little village of Salem (later called Jerusalem) on his victory march to the south.

"And Melchizedek king of Salem brought out bread

and wine; now he was a priest of God Most High. And he blessed him and said, 'Blessed be Abram of God Most High, Possessor of heaven and earth; and blessed be God Most High, Who has delivered your enemies into your hand.' And he [Abram] gave him a tenth of all'' (Genesis 14:18-20).

Such are the scanty facts regarding this person about whom the writer of Hebrews makes so much. There is a second reference to this majestic figure, explaining the Messiah will be ''. . . a priest forever according to the order of Melchizedek'' (Psalm 110:4), a prophecy the writer of Hebrews sees as being perfectly fulfilled by Christ and His ministry. Beyond what is written in Genesis 14 and Psalm 110, there is nothing.

At this point it is absolutely imperative to note that in developing his argument our author is not talking about Melchizedek, but about Jesus. The book of Hebrews is about Jesus. Who Jesus was. What Jesus did. All Jesus means in time and eternity. Remember that, lest you focus on the wrong figure. Everything said about Melchizedek is, in reality, a statement about Jesus. Unless you move past Melchizedek to Jesus, you'll miss the whole point.

As already suggested, Melchizedek is a prototype of Christ. He serves one and only one purpose; that is, to prove the existence of another order of priesthood that is older, superior, and, thus, transcendent over both the Levitical priesthood and the law which rests upon it.

Once our author has made his point, he drops Melchizedek and focuses on Jesus. As Charles R. Erdman explains, this majestic figure stands for one short scene on the pages of scripture to establish the validity, dignity and efficacy of Christ's priesthood, then disappears forever into the mystery from which he emerged.

Now, the writer of Hebrews was a most ingenious

preacher. Chapter 7 is really a sermon on Psalm 110:4—" 'Thou art a priest forever according to the order of Melchizedek.' " He starts his sermon by restating the facts recorded in Genesis 14. "For this Melchizedek, king of Salem, priest of the Most High God, who met Abraham as he was returning from the slaughter of the kings and blessed him, to whom also Abraham apportioned a tenth part of all the spoils . . ." (7:1,2). From this bare beginning and by means of etymology and typology, the writer of Hebrews fashions a most fascinating rationale for the priesthood of Jesus.

First, he gives a lesson in etymology, the study of words and their origins. He points out that Melchizedek means "king of righteousness." And, being king of Salem, meaning "peace," Melchizedek was also "king of peace." With great care, the Holy Spirit has guarded even the apparently insignificant matter of the order of the names by which this prototype of Christ is called. First, king of righteousness. Second, king of peace.

This order is in perfect harmony with other scripture. For instance, "The work of righteousness will be peace, and the service of righteousness, quietness and confidence [assurance] forever" (Isaiah 32:17). Notice which comes first: Righteousness, then peace. Righteousness, then assurance.

Earlier in the book of Hebrews we are informed that, because Jesus loved righteousness, the heavenly Father anointed Him with the oil of gladness (1:9). The scripture makes it clear that the happiness, security, and peace we so feverishly seek in various and sundry ways are only possible through obedience. Righteousness and joy are wed. Righteousness and assurance are wed. So, too, are righteousness and peace. In each instance, righteousness comes first!

Is it possible that you, like many others, have put the

cart before the horse? Is it possible you have pursued happiness, security, and peace, only to find your dreams lying like bits of broken rainbow about your feet? The solution is to put first things first. Pursue righteousness. Then the assurance, joy and peace you're seeking will come as an automatic outcropping of obedience. The priesthood of this prototype of Christ was righteous, peaceful and, thus, royal in the highest and truest sense of that word.

Continuing his sermon, the writer of Hebrews moves from etymology, the study of words, to typology, the study of symbols. He gives us a most interesting lesson in one kind of Biblical interpretation. He argues both from what the Bible says and from what the Bible does not say. When studying God's written word, remember: What is included and what is excluded are both significant.

From the silence of scripture, he points out the permanence of Melchizedek's priesthood. From the statements of scripture, he emphasizes the preeminence of his priesthood. Both of these—permanence and preeminence—serve to illustrate the durability and dignity of Christ's priesthood. First, he builds an argument around what the Bible doesn't say about Melchizedek's ancestry and progeny. He is "without father, without mother, without genealogy. . ."(7:3).

Genealogy, the study of family pedigrees, is not too important to us, but it was absolutely vital to the Old Testament priesthood. If a person could not prove an unbroken descent from Aaron, he could not qualify as a Levitical priest. To be part of the Old Testament priesthood, one had to be a particular strand of "true blue Jew."

This is the point the writer of Hebrews makes when he speaks of those who were priests according to a "law of physical requirement. . ." (7:16).

The striking difference between the Levitical priesthood, and that of Melchizedek and therefore, Christ, is that the former rested solely upon heredity. A boy became a priest because his pappy was.

Just before Aaron died, Moses took him to the summit of Mount Hor, removed his priestly garments and put them on Eleazar, Aaron's son (Numbers 20:28). Later, when Eleazar died, the mantle succeeded to his son, Phinehas. And so it went, generation after generation. From the time of Aaron to the destruction of the second temple in A.D. 70, there were 83 high priests who functioned solely upon the basis of heredity.

Melchizedek could not claim priesthood by human succession (7:3). Neither could the Christian's high priest, Jesus. Both were priests by divine fiat. The silence of scripture regarding the genealogy of Melchizedek does not suggest he was some sort of biological anomaly who, like Topsy, just grew. Rather, the absence of any information about his ancestry or progeny, his life or death, is to emphasize the uniqueness of his priesthood. It was not based on who his father was, but upon the spiritual qualifications of the man himself. Thus, it was a priesthood of enduring nature.

Using Melchizedek as a prototype of Christ, the writer of Hebrews then argues his case for the permanence of Christ's priesthood. Like "Mel's," the priesthood of Jesus is not based upon heredity. Jesus was of the tribe of Judah, not the tribe of Levi. Thus, like that of his prototype, the priesthood of Jesus rested on the character and quality of the man Himself. Furthermore, because Jesus died, rose again, and ascended to heaven, He now reigns as Priest without end. Thus, His priesthood is absolutely permanent.

From this point made by the silence of scripture, the writer of Hebrews turns to the statements of scripture.

Based upon what the Bible does say, he emphasized the preeminence of Melchizedek and, thus, the preeminence of Jesus. "See how great he is! Abraham, the patriarch, gave him a tithe of the spoils." And Melchizedek "blessed [him] who had the promises" (7:6).

This was not an effort to deprecate Abraham, but to elevate Melchizedek. Simply put, the argument runs as follows: Melchizedek is greater than Abraham because he (Melchizedek) blessed the patriarch and accepted his tithes, both acts implying superior standing and authority. Levi was the great-grandson of Abraham. As explained in beautiful Hebrew picture language, he was "still in the loins" (7:10) of Abraham at the time of this incident.

Therefore, Melchizedek is greater than Levi. Symbolically, he collected tithes from Levi through Abraham, again implying greater standing and authority. Since Christ's priesthood is "according to the order of Melchizedek," who was superior to Levi, Christ's priestly ministry, too, is greater than that of the Levitical priests. Ipso facto, Christ, the Christian's high priest, enjoys preeminence as well as permanence.

At this point, the argument becomes somewhat more sophisticated. If this line of reasoning seems a bit strained, remember that, to the devout Jew, the ceremonial law was everything with a capitol "E". To assault the ceremonial law and those who practiced it, to suggest that the law was inadequate, was to attack the jugular vein of Judaism. Yet, this is precisely what the writer of Hebrews does.

"Now if perfection was through the Levitical priesthood (for on the basis of it the people received the Law), what further need was there for another priest to arise acccording to the order of Melchizedek, and not be designated according to the order of Aaron?" (7:11).

The key word here is "perfection." Had it been attainable through the Old Testament priests and practices, there would be no need for Jesus. But, as everyone knew, the ceremonial law and the Old Testament priests who performed it could not attain this goal. They could challenge people to perfection, but they could not in any way empower people to achieve perfection. They could not cause a man to stop sinning, for instance. They could not make a man perfect, in either God's eyes or his own. That's why the old order was useless, for "the Law made nothing perfect" (7:19a). Therefore, it had to go.

God, who had given it and used it as a temporary measure of dealing with His people, now removed it. "For, on the one hand, there is a setting aside of a former commandment because of its weakness and uselessness (for the Law made nothing perfect), and on the other hand there is a bringing in of a better hope, through which we draw near to God" (7:18,19).

A new day had come. The day of spiritual rebirth when, through Christ, a person became a new creature (II Corinthians 5:17). When he was, in fact, perfect in the eyes of God. And, even greater, was given the very life of God Himself, whereby he had power to stop sinning. To live creatively, rather than destructively.

At this point, the writer of Hebrews draws his conclusion: Jesus is our hope. Jesus is "a priest according to the order of Melchizedek" (7:17). Instead of belonging to that old order described as having many priests who died (7:23), who bequeathed their mantle to another without ever having helped one man know with finality he was right with God; the Lord Jesus belongs to a new priesthood, operating under a new covenant, in which there is one Priest who lives forever, whose authority and mantle are non-transferable (7:24). A Priest who, by offering Himself as the perfect sacrifice, makes it possible for those who put their trust in Him to be perfect in God's sight, and Who gives them the privilege of drawing near to God with confidence and joy (7:25).

"For it was fitting that we should have such a high priest, holy, innocent, undefiled, separated from sinners and exalted above the heavens; who does not need daily, like those high priests, to offer up sacrifices, first for His own sins, and then for the sins of the people, because this He did once for all when He offered up Himself. For the Law appoints men as high priests who are weak, but the word of the oath, which came after the Law, appoints a Son, made perfect forever" (7:26-28). What a grand Amen to this tremendous statement regarding the permanence and preeminence of Jesus!

Let's look at the marvelous statement regarding the peerless and impeccable character of Jesus Christ (7:26). In His relationship toward God, He was holy. In His relationship toward men, He was harmless. In His relationship toward Himself, He was undefiled. Jesus was "separated from sinners"; that is, different from the rest of us. Often, when tempted, we fall. But Jesus, tempted in all ways, remained unsullied by sin.

As a result, He's "exalted above the heavens" (7:26). What a wonderful example of Hebrew picture speech and hyperbole! Today we might say, "Man, He's outa sight!" "He's the greatest!" "He's out of this world!" Our first-century penman said, He's "exalted above the heavens."

And He was. He is. Jesus is completely and forever able to save (7:25) all who respond to His gentle invitation. "Come to Me" (Matthew 11:28a). Him "who comes to Me I will certainly not cast out" (John 6:37).

What does all this mean to you? Why should you care that Christ is a priest after the order of Melchizedek? The implications, as I see them, are four. Jesus wants to save you. Free you. Satisfy you. So He can use you.

JESUS WANTS TO SAVE YOU

When Melchizedek met Abram coming home on his victory march, he met a man who, by most human standards, had every right to enjoy the sweet taste of victory. The temptation was to do so by watering down his witness for God. The lesson God wanted Abram to learn was this: He didn't have to go to war to improve his Dun and Bradstreet rating. Nor did he need to enrich himself through the misery of others.

"God is your provider and protector," Melchizedek seems to say. "It is He who has helped you gain the victory in this recent fracas. You are not a self-made man, Abram; you never will be. You are a man blessed by God to be a blessing. Everything you are, everything you hope to be, everything you become, will be the result of His action in your life. So now, in this moment of small victory, remember to Whom the glory is due."

To his credit, Abram, who later became famous for his spiritual sensitivity, immediately recognized the import of Melchizedek's words. And he gave a tithe of the treasures he had recovered from the kings. This may seem a strange thing for Abram to do. But it was the tithing decision which kept Abram's purpose clear and his priorities straight. By tithing, he fixed in his mind the truth about ownership and stewardship. For, to give a tenth is to acknowledge God owns the whole. It is to admit one is only a temporary user of that which belongs to God.

Through the act of tithing, which God has been using for a long, long time as a means of molding men, the Lord was able, in a most profound and intensely personal way, to "save" Abram. In this manner, God helped Abram to win the greatest of all victories: the victory over

Abram! Abram was, in effect, saved from glorification of self. Fortified spiritually through this internal conquest, and physically through the bread and wine Melchizedek gave him, Abram was able to turn his back on the blandishments of the king of Sodom. As a result, no man would ever be able to say, "I have made Abram rich" (Genesis 14:23b). If the patriarch were to become an economic success, as in later life he did, the glory would always go to God.

Through His minister, Melchizedek, God met Abram at a crucial spiritual crossroad. Because of Abram's response, God was able to give him the greatest of all victories—the victory over self. And, what God did for Abraham through Melchizedek, He wants to do for you through Jesus. He wants to save you from yourself. He wants to give you the greatest of all victories—the victory over self. He wants to help you, as a Christian, keep your purpose clear and your priorities straight.

Until you gain the victory over self, learn to trust God and acknowledge Him as your patron and provider, you will be looking for an angle. You will be searching for an edge. An advantage which gives you a little extra leverage in the game of dog-eat-dog. But God says, "No! Trust Me. Remember, it is I who give you the physical strength and the mental acumen, the time and talent, to win in this warfare against the confederacy of world, flesh and devil.

"Therefore, play it straight. By My rules. Even though it may seem costly. In the long run, the personal, spiritual, and perhaps material rewards will be great. Remember, as it was with Abraham, so it is with you. Tithing is not My way of getting your money. It is My way of getting *you*. It is My method of shaping you into someone I can trust and use, because you are someone to whom Jesus has given the greatest of all victories: the victory over self!"

JESUS WANTS TO FREE YOU

Our Lord not only wants to save you from yourself; He wants to free you from the preoccupying power of a sinful past. Several years ago, I stood facing the ark with the members of a Hebrew congregation. When the Rabbi took the Torah, the Jewish Law, out of the ark and held it on his shoulder for a moment, I felt as if I were standing on holy ground. I remember thinking to myself, "The world needs that law right now. It needs to know and obey that law. It needs to heed the warning of that law."

But, as the Rabbi tenderly put the Torah back in the ark, it suddenly hit me! The law is not what the world really needs. The law can do no more for folk today than it did for folk in Old Testament times. It may raise man's standards, but it cannot impart power to the people to achieve those standards. It may clarify one's duties, but it cannot awaken the love to do those duties.

The law may threaten, but it cannot change. It cannot turn despair into hope. The more one reads the law, the more he is aware of what he hasn't done. The law may widen the gap between a man and God, but the law can do nothing to bridge that gap. The law never made anyone perfect (7:19). It has only served to accentuate the fact of one's imperfection.

Jesus does the opposite. He not only points out your imperfections, He gives you power to do something about them. He not only saves you from yourself, He frees you from the preoccupying power of unresolved guilt so, as a saved sinner, you are free to be the blessing you were blessed to be.

When you come to Jesus and, in an attitude of genuine repentance say, "This is sin. I don't *want* to want to go on sinning anymore," the Lord Jesus gives you His righteousness. At that moment, you inherit His past. His past is perfect! You stand before God as if you had never sinned. Whiter than snow (Isaiah 1:18).

If, after that moment of initial commitment to Christ, you sin again, as we all do, you need only come to Christ in a fresh act of repentance. Each time you do so, the field of your past, which is now whiter than snow, expands. Day by day. Week by week. As long as life lasts.

JESUS WANTS TO SATISFY YOU

The Master not only saves you and frees you, He also satisfies you. Because He makes you perfect in God's sight and frees you from the preoccupying power of a sinful past, you can now draw near to God with confidence and joy, knowing you'll be received.

The Old Testament priesthood and law suffered from a vexing weakness. They could arouse within folk a longing for access to God. They could stimulate, inspire, even express, this deepest hunger of the human heart. But, they could do absolutely nothing to satisfy this hunger. Jesus can. He saves you. Frees you. Even more, He satisfies you. His priesthood, like that of Melchizedek, is not temporary but eternal. It is not earthly but heavenly. It is not based upon human succession, but is sealed by an oath of God. Therefore, there will never come a time when His ministry on your behalf becomes ineffective.

You will never turn to Jesus for help or hope and fail to find Him alive and active. He saves "to the uttermost" (7:25, KJV). Which means more than saving you from every kind of sin, though that's true. Even more wonderful, it means saving you forevermore! The ministry of Christ on your behalf will never cease. The door to God's presence is ever open. You will never find a "vacancy" or "job open" sign hung over the place of His employment.

JESUS WANTS TO USE YOU

Why does He do all this? Why does Jesus save you from yourself? Free you from the preoccupying power of a sinful past? Why does He go to such lengths to satisfy you by being exactly what you need, when and where you need it? Because He wants to use you. He wants you to be about your Father's business. Not butting in where you're unwanted and unwelcome. But being awake and sensitive to the opportunities all around you for witness and service in Jesus' name.

God's purpose in sending His Son into the world was not solely to make saints out of sinners, but having done so, to make servants out of saints. That's what He ever so much wants to make of you—a servant. A person who knows Whom he represents and, understanding Christ's qualifications and capacity to help, will be to his contemporary world everything Jesus would be if He were physically here Himself!

A big order? You bet it is. But all it requires are the dual ingredients of genuine humility and sheer obedience. As one girl put it:

> They tell me
> an angel
> couldn't fit
> the job description
> on this assignment,
> so why did You hand it to me?
>
> And—when
> do You want me
> to start?[3]

4

OUR HOPE: Jesus Completes a New Contract

Hebrews 8

NOW the main point in what has been said is this: we have such a high priest, who has taken His seat at the right hand of the throne of the Majesty in the heavens, ²a minister in the sanctuary, and in the true tabernacle, which the Lord pitched, not man. ³For every high priest is appointed to offer both gifts and sacrifices; hence it is necessary that this high priest also have something to offer.

⁴Now if He were on earth, He would not be a priest at all, since there are those who offer the gifts according to the Law; ⁵who serve a copy and shadow of the heavenly things, just as Moses was warned by God when he was about to erect the tabernacle; for, "See," He says, "that you make all things according to the pattern which was shown you on the mountain." ⁶But now He has obtained a more excellent ministry, by as much as He is also the mediator of a better covenant, which has been enacted on better promises. ⁷For if that first covenant had been faultless, there would have been no occasion sought for a second.

⁸For finding fault with them, He says,

"Behold, days are coming, says the Lord,

When I will effect a new convenant
With the house of Israel and with the house
of Judah;
[9]*Not like the covenant which I made with*
their fathers
On the day when I took them by the hand
To lead them out of the land of Egypt;
For they did not continue in My covenant,
And I did not care for them, says the Lord.
[10]*For this is the covenant that I will make with*
the house of Israel
After those days, says the Lord:
I will put My laws into their minds,
And will write them upon their hearts.
And I will be their God,
And they shall be My people.
"And they shall not teach every one his
fellowcitizen,
And every one his brother, saying, 'Know
the Lord,'
For all shall know Me,
From the least to the greatest of them.
[12]*For I will be merciful to their iniquities,*
And I will remember their sins no more."
[13]*When He said, "A new covenant," He has*
made the first obsolete. But whatever is becoming
obsolete and growing old is ready to disappear.

When you receive Jesus Christ as Saviour, the devil loses you for eternity. As far as life after death is concerned, the issue is settled. You belong to God. Having failed with Plan A, the devil then moves to Plan B. Having lost you for eternity, he seeks to capture you for time.

One of his most effective means of achieving this objective is to infect you with a chronic case of me-on-my-mind-itis. This is a dreadful, debilitating disease. Among other things, it causes you to develop an allergy to yourself. Usually it springs from unresolved guilt feelings which the devil cleverly uses to generate a towering sense of self-loathing and a loss of self-love.

By making you feel worthless, he succeeds in making you feel useless. Instead of being turned on for Jesus, you become turned in on yourself. You are neutralized as a vital force for God here on earth, and Satan, who lost you for eternity, succeeds in gaining you for time.

Now God, who made you and knows you far better than you know yourself, is sensitive to your vulnerability in this area. Long before you ever were, He prepared a creative means of handling guilt so you could be free to be the blessing you were meant to be. His plan is called *forgiveness*.

To grasp the wonder and thoroughness of God's plan, we need a brief history lesson. About 4,000 years ago, God made a covenant with Abram and his offspring, promising to bless them and use them to be a blessing, on the express condition that they obey Him (Genesis 12:1-3). Through a series of subsequent and quite marvelous events, in which the hand of God is clearly seen, this small tribe of people migrated to Egypt where, in a kind of geographic isolationism, they took on the rough-hewn shape of a nation.

For a period of time they were subjected to the indignities of slavery, but this only strengthened their resolve to be free. At long last, they were released from the yoke of bondage, and they set out on their pilgrimage to the Promised Land. During the course of their journey, God gave them certain stabilizing influences. One was the moral law, or Ten Commandments. Another was a system of sacrifices which they were to offer when guilty of forsaking these Commandments.

Subsequent to the giving of the law, God reiterated His earlier covenant (Genesis 12:1-4; Genesis 15:5), promising to bless the offspring of Abraham if they obeyed Him (Exodus 23:20-30). The covenant between God and man is different from most contracts worked out by two people who meet on more or less the same level. Two equals can haggle and argue over the terms of the agreement, each trying to make the best possible deal. But, as William Barclay explains, with God and man no such relationship can occur, for man is not and never will be on the same plane as God. "In any relationship between God and man, it is God alone who can take the initiative, and man can only accept or refuse both the offer and the conditions of God. Man cannot argue or bargain with God as he can with other men."[1]

In this particular instance, the people of God agreed to the terms of God. The covenant relationship was entered into. "Then Moses came and recounted to the people all the words of the Lord and all the ordinances; and all the people answered with one voice, and said, 'All the words which the Lord has spoken we will do!' And Moses wrote down all the words of the Lord. Then he arose early in the morning, and built an altar at the foot of the mountain with twelve pillars for the twelve tribes of Israel. And he sent young men of the sons of Israel, and they offered burnt offerings and sacrificed young bulls as peace offerings to the Lord. And Moses took half of the blood and put it in basins, and the other half of the blood he sprinkled on the altar.

''Then he took the Book of the Covenant and read it in the hearing of the people; and they said, 'All that the Lord has spoken we will do, and we will be obedient!' '' So Moses took the blood and sprinkled it on the people, and said, 'Behold, the blood of the covenant, which the Lord has made with you in accordance with all these words' '' (Exodus 24:3-8).

Here's the gist of it: God took the initiative and singled out Israel. He promised to bless her so that she might be a blessing. The condition was obedience. The people agreed to this stipulation. A sacrifice was made. The covenant was ratified in blood. The relationship between God and Israel was sealed.

Unfortunately, it didn't work out as planned. Man proved incapable of keeping the law, and a giant snafu occurred. Each breach of the law created a breach in the relationship. To mend it, God instituted the plan of atonement (Leviticus 16). A whole hierarchy of priests and apparatus of sacrifice were instituted. The idea was that, when the proper sacrifice was made, this poor, sinful, alienated people could at least receive a temporary sense of hope and healing.

Again, all the bases seemed to be covered. But, unfortunately, another flaw appeared. The blood of animals was inadequate. It could not then and cannot now take away sin (Hebrews 10:4). It cannot cleanse the human conscience (9:9). The organized priesthood and ritual of animal sacrifice were unable to accomplish what they were meant to do. They could not maintain the relationship between God and man.

Put simply, the covenant failed. So God interceded again and in the "fulness of time" (Galatians 4:4,5), He sent His Son into the world to do what no one and nothing else could do: establish a *lasting* relationship between the Father and His wayward children.

Aware of the inadequacies of the old covenant, and captivated by the all-eclipsing radiance of Christ, many first-century Jews turned to Jesus. During the early years of their Christian life, buoyed by the euphoric lift of first love, they did not find it too difficult to get by without the aid of temple, priest and visible sacrifice. But, as time passed and their early enthusiasm began to wane, many of these Hebrew Christians began to wonder what to do about the problem of me-on-my-mind-itis.

Even though they had accepted Christ as Saviour, they still had a problem with sin. They still succumbed to temptation. With each moral defeat, Satan, who had lost them for eternity, moved in to capture them for time. Taking the normal guilt mechanism God had put inside them as a protective device, Satan twisted and turned it into a tool with which to torture them with feelings of guilt, remorse, shame, self-loathing and uselessness. By so doing, he effectively neutralized them as a vital force for God on earth.

What were they to do? The Christian faith has no temple. No sacrificial system. No priestly order. How does Christianity propose to deal with the disease of me-on-my-mind-itis when it has no high priest to offer the proper sacrifice in the Holy of Holies?

The writer of Hebrews tells them they are worrying about a problem that doesn't exist: "Now the main point in what has been said is this: we have such a high priest, who has taken His seat at the right hand of the throne of the Majesty in the heavens''(8:1). He then goes on to make three powerful points. First, a true high priest must have a place in which to minister, and Christ, the Christian's high priest, has such a place. Second, a true high priest must have a sacrifice to offer, and Christ, the Christian's high priest, has made the best of all sacrifices. Third, a true high priest mediates between God and man on the basis of an agreement or covenant which God has set up, and the Christian's high priest does just that.

So much for the history lesson. Before we go on to see what all this has to do with you and Satan's Plan B, let's quickly review what we've learned thus far from the book of Hebrews.

Chapters 1:1 through 5:10 are devoted to proving Jesus is greater than the prophets, angels, Moses, Joshua and Aaron. The wee section consisting of 5:11 through 6:3 gives us the interpretive key which unlocks this spiritual treasure chest.

The first half of chapter 6 and, as we shall learn later, the last half of chapter 10, issue stern warnings against certain deadly dangers which can lead Christians astray. Between these two caution lights is the marvelous parenthesis with which we are now concerned. It consists of chapters 7 through 9, and describes the utterly adequate intercessory ministry of Jesus, the Christian's high priest. *Christ is God's provision for our failing and falling.* He is the Great Physician who can heal us from me-on-my-mind-itis. He is the all-sufficient Saviour who can free us to be the blessing we were blessed to be.

In chapter 7, too, as we have already learned, our author proves Christ's priesthood is greater than that of Aaron or Levi. It is by divine appointment, not human ancestry. It is supported by a godly oath which has never been revoked. In chapter 8, to which we will turn in a moment, he shows Christ's ministry is also greater. It is spiritual and eternal, not earthly and temporary. In chapter 9:1 through 10:18, the writer of Hebrews shows how Christ's sacrifice is greater. It was one sacrifice, not many. It was offered once for all, not over and over again.

Our author is attempting to reassure these early Christians, who by tradition and experience have become accustomed to a visible temple, priest and sacrifice, that these Old Testament provisions were provisional. They were temporary forerunners of things to come. They pointed beyond themselves to that which would be final and complete.

To nail down his argument, the writer of Hebrews offers two illustrations. The first has to do with the scene of Christ's ministry. "Now the main point in what has been said is this: we have such a high priest, who has taken His seat at the right hand of the throne of the Majesty in the heavens, a minister in the sanctuary, and in the true tabernacle which the Lord pitched, not man. For every high priest is appointed to offer both gifts and sacrifices; hence it is necessary that this high priest also have something to offer.

"Now if He were on earth, He would not be a priest at all, since there are those who offer the gifts according to the Law; who serve a copy and shadow of the heavenly things, just as Moses was warned by God when he was about to erect the tabernacle; for, 'See,' He says, 'that you make all things according to the pattern which was shown you on the mountain.' But now He has obtained a more excellent ministry, by as much as He is also the mediator of a better covenant, which has been enacted on better promises" (8:4-6).

His line of logic is quite simple. Every high priest officiates in some sanctuary. Christ, the Christian's high priest, officiates in the true sanctuary of which the tabernacle in the wilderness was just a copy or reasonable facsimile. We all know, for instance, that long before a house is built, it exists in the mind of the architect. What later appears on a plot of ground somewhere is just a copy, more or less imperfect, of the true house which eye has not seen and human hand can never touch.

The tabernacle in the wilderness was just such a copy, more or less imperfect, of the *true* sanctuary in heaven. It represented realities, known only to God, which He wanted to reveal, at least in part, to His children. Because Christ, the Christian's high priest, operates in the real sanctuary, not a replica of the real, His ministry is superior to that of earthly priests. He deals with pure reality rather than mere ritual or fading replicas.

Does this suggest to you, as it does to me, that we ought to take another look at what we think is real? For the most part, we are committed to things we can see, hear, taste, touch and smell. If our senses confirm their existence, we say they're real. Earth is our true home, we think. Heaven, if it exists at all, is uncertain and vague. There may be life after death, but we had better follow the safe course and eat, drink and be merry for this may be all there is. The Bible in general, and Hebrews in particular, says it's the other way around. If anything is tentative and fragile, it is the world in which we now live.

The Lord Jesus gave us some mighty good advice when He said, "And do not fear those who kill the body, but are unable to kill the soul;" that is, your true self (Matthew 10:28). We would be wise to heed His words. We lavish far too much time, attention and money on that which is purely temporary. We overlook the eternal. How sad! God wants to give us the Pearl of Great Price. Yet often we settle for glass beads.

For his second illustration, our author directs our attention from the scene of Christ's ministry to the substance of His ministry which centers around a new contract. It is a truism that a contract is only as good as the character of the people who sign it. We might say, therefore, that the old covenant was not worth the rock it was written on. One of the signatories—man—was and is wholly incapable of keeping his end of the bargain.

This signaled the necessity for something new. Something deeper and more durable than a merely external agreement which was sure to be broken sooner or later.

It is the assertion of the writer of Hebrews; in verses 7-13, that this something new has been worked out and made available by Christ. It is a new covenant, which is to be in the believer's mind and written on his heart. All believers will know God—know Him intimately—because of Christ. The new covenant makes the old covenant obsolete, because it had failed.

The old covenant failed because of the frailty of man. It was not the law God found fault with; it was the people. He finds "fault with them" (8:8). Actually, the old covenant had been abandoned by both parties. "For they did not continue in My covenant, and I did not care for them" (8:9).

There had been a complete breakdown in the apparatus for release from me-on-my-mind-itis. Prophets who lived under the old covenant recognized this flaw and predicted a new covenant (Jeremiah 31:31-34). This new covenant would not be written on tablets of stone as was the covenant at Sinai. It would not be dependent upon animal sacrifice. And, most amazing of all, it would not be conditioned by human effort or response. It would entail an entirely new and utterly thrilling relationship, initiated by God, which would make possible what the old covenant could not do.

The old covenant was conditional. Its validity and continuance depended upon man's obedience. "If you will," God had stipulated in the old agreement. In the new covenant, the word "if" does not occur once. Instead, repeatedly in verses 10 and 12 we have God's promise, "I will." "I will make a covenant . . ."; "I will put my laws into their minds . . ."; "I will be their God . . ."; "I will be merciful . . ."; "I will remember their sins no more."

This *is* a better covenant, for now God doesn't ask you to promise Him anything. All He asks is that you believe His promises! That may seem too good to be true. But that's the nature of the Good News. That's the source of our hope. Jesus completes a new contract.

To borrow Paul's words, "For what the Law could not do, weak as it was through the flesh, God did: sending His own Son in the likeness of sinful flesh and as an offering for sin, He condemned sin in the flesh" (Romans 8:3). The defect in the old covenant did not lie in the law itself. The law was good enough. The defect lay in the weakness of the flesh (Romans 8:3).

The same would be true of the new covenant if Christ had not fulfilled the conditions for us. You and I are no better, no stronger, no more resistant to temptation than Israel of old. But Jesus paid it all. He has taken our place. In our name, He has fulfilled the essential stipulation of perfect trust and obedience. Thus, God is able to deal with us on these liberal terms, permitting us to share in the blessings and benefits of this better covenant based on better promises.

This takes the pressure off us. We no longer have to *do* anything to secure salvation. We merely trust in Him, believing that what God has promised He is able to perform. Our relationship with God is firm and final. It can never be broken. We are saved forevermore. Satan has lost the battle for eternity. So, in an effort to harass us in this life, he moves to Plan B. He uses sin to destroy our *fellowship* with God. But, if we learn to use the provisions of our faith, we can lick him on that score, too. Thus we beat him both ways! Hallelujah!

What are the practical applications of this for contemporary Christians? I see four: You can be yourself through the power of Jesus. Or you'll be a goose egg without God. You're blessed beyond belief. So you can be turned on instead of turned in.

YOU CAN BE YOURSELF THROUGH THE POWER OF JESUS

The problem with the old arrangement—the old covenant—is that the human material with which God had to work just wasn't capable of keeping the law. What was needed was a new nature. This is precisely what Christ provides. When He moves into your life, He installs a new kind of guidance system. It is internal rather than external. Spiritual rather than legal. Under the new covenant, God says, ". . . I will put My laws into their minds, and I will write them upon their hearts . . ." (8:10).

I was a Christian many years before I discovered this wonderful truth. I took the Christian life seriously. I wanted very much to be like Jesus and continually fell short. I was trying to be Jesus through the power of John Lavender. It just wouldn't work. One day I read where Jesus explained He could do nothing on His own (John 5:19,30). That hit me like a ton of bricks.

If Christ couldn't do it alone, what hope was there for me? I was really in the soup. Shortly thereafter, I discovered the great principle of, "Christ *in* [me], the hope of glory" (Colossians 1:27). I was never meant to live the Christian life under my own power. I was only meant to permit Christ to live His life through me. So I stopped trying to be Jesus through the power of John Lavender and decided to be John Lavender through the power of Jesus! Things have gone much better ever since.

You can be yourself through the power of Jesus. Among the many gifts God gives you when you turn yourself over to Him is the gift of yourself. Your true self. The self you want and were meant to be. Under the terms of the contract Christ has completed, there are hidden springs of inner spiritual insight and energy which, if you are willing, can propel you down the right path. You can be you through the power of Jesus. But—

YOU'LL BE A GOOSE EGG WITHOUT GOD

The new covenant is not only spiritual; it is personal. Under the terms of this contract, the heavenly Father says, ". . . I will be their God, and they shall be My people" (8:10).

A little boy who had been listening to the sad state of world affairs as reported on the evening newscast, went to bed and in his nighty-night prayer was heard to say, "Dear God, take care of Mommy and Daddy. And my little sister. And Grandma. And please, dear God, be sure to take care of Yourself, 'cause if anything happens to You, we're sunk!"

The little boy grasped an important truth. When the heavenly Father promises to be your God, He is promising to be your everything. Dr. Richard H. Bube, Professor of Physics at Stanford University, poses an interesting question. If God turned Himself off, what would happen? The good professor is bright enough to know philosophically and theologically such a thing is not possible. He only asks the question to force us to face our true feelings about the significance of God.

He says there are only four possible answers to the question. First, *nothing would happen*. Those who give that answer indicate they do not believe God exists at all. A second answer is that, *while nothing physical would happen, morally there would be a serious breakdown*. People would become less loving and more hateful. Less giving and more greedy. Less social and more egocentric. Those who give this answer indicate they do not see God as having anything to do with the physical order. If He exists at all, it is merely for the sake of moral values.

Third, *there would be a gradual disintegration of life*. Slowly, but surely, a breakdown in the physical order would occur. Those who give this answer reveal a belief in God as a vague, impersonal life force out there somewhere controlling the physical universe, but wholly unconcerned with man in a personal way.

Or, fourth, *the whole shebang would stop instantly*. Dr. Bube suggests this is the only conceivable answer for people of the Book. To illustrate his point he draws upon an analogy made by Dr. D. M. MacKay of Keele University in England. A story is being acted out on the screen of a television set. The people are loving each other. Hating each other. Fighting each other. Helping each other. When the TV set is turned off, the people don't begin to stop loving each other. They don't gradually stop hating. Or fighting. Or helping each other. There is not a slow disintegration of the action being depicted there. Not at all. The whole story stops—immediately—period!

The same is true with God. He is your everything. Without Him there would be no you. If God were to turn Himself off, the whole shebang would come to a grinding halt. Instantly. For He is your everything! Keep that fact on the first row of your mind. "With God all things are possible'' (Matthew 19:26). He can provide you with the power needed to become what you were meant to be. But apart from Him, you're in trouble.

God cannot turn Himself off. But you can turn Him off. You can block Him out of your life. You can decide to go it alone. But, the moment you do, you're in difficulty. He is your everything. And, while you can be yourself through the power of Jesus, you'll be a goose egg without God.

YOU ARE BLESSED BEYOND BELIEF

The new covenant is not only spiritual and personal, it's universal: "For all shall know Me, from the least to the greatest of them" (8:11). Under the new arrangement which Christ has completed, there is no privileged class of people. God reveals Himself to all of the redeemed. Not just to a select few. Christ and the knowledge of Him become the least common denominator, binding all believers in Christian love.

Nor is there anyone standing between you and God. This knowledge of Him and His will for your life is not vicarious knowledge gained through a preacher. Or priest. Or teacher. It is a personal knowledge. The Lord Himself speaks and reveals Himself to you.

If one great truth shines through the book of Hebrews it is this: Christ has opened a way for everyone to enter into a new and dear relationship with God. Having that relationship, you are blessed beyond belief.

YOU CAN BE TURNED ON INSTEAD OF TURNED IN

Thus, we came full circle. Satan not only fails with Plan A, losing you for eternity when you meet Jesus at

Calvary. He also fails with Plan B, losing you in time when, as a saved sinner, you meet Christ in an honest prayer of confession and repentance.

The new covenant is not only spiritual, personal and universal, it is final. "For I will be merciful to their iniquities. And I will remember their sins no more" (8:12). What incredible good news that is! God never says, "I told you so." God never flings the past in your face. God never dredges up old mistakes and rehashes old sins. When God forgives, He forgets. Not because He takes sin lightly. He takes it very seriously. It cost Him His Son. But God forgives and forgets because He wants you to be free to be the blessing you were blessed to be.

God knows unresolved guilt is like a toothache. Distracting. Unnerving. Debilitating. It is impossible for you to be cured of me-on-my-mind-itis if you're constantly confronted with the harvest of past sins. That's why God says, "There is therefore now no condemnation for those who are in Christ Jesus" (Romans 8:1). None. Absolutely none.

When, as a saved sinner, you come to Jesus with your sin, confess it, repent of it, receive God's cleansing from it—it's over! From that point on, God doesn't want you to waste five seconds in remorse over it. He wants you to get on with the business of being a blessing. If God doesn't condemn you, how can you possibly condemn yourself?

Satan would have you see yourself as a dirty, rotten sinner. If you accept his appraisal, you will slip into self-loathing and be utterly useless to the Kingdom. God wants you to see yourself as a dirty, rotten *forgiven* sinner. And, if you can see yourself in that light, you will be liberated from the disease of me-on-my-mind-itis. You will be lifted by the creative power of wholesome self-love to a new operational level. You will become a dynamic force for healing in a broken world.

If you forget everything else I have written, remember this: *As a forgiven sinner-saint, you are free to do anything God has in mind for you.* You may feel that, because of sin and failure as a Christian, you have forfeited your right to serve the Lord. Don't you believe it! As a forgiven Christian, you are free to do anything God has in mind for you. Get hold of that great truth. Let that great truth get hold of you. You will never be the same. You'll be turned on instead of turned in. And when that happens, Satan will be whipped on both fronts—in time and in eternity.

> Clay ship idling
> on its launching pad
> vapor leaking from its valves
> power to soar
> cancelled
> by the gravitation of self.
>
> Begin the countdown, Lord!
> Order all systems go
> Free this tethered craft
> fill each fuel cell
> ignite it with Your life
> then lift it off
> give it full thrust
> execute the burns
> maneuver it into orbit
> stabilize the gyrations
> accomplish Your mission.[1]

—*Beverly Caviness*

5

OUR HOPE: Jesus Is All You Need

Hebrews 9:1-15

NOW even the first covenant had regulations of divine worship and the earthly sanctuary. ²For there was a tabernacle prepared, the outer one, in which were the lampstand and the table and the sacred bread; this is called the holy place. ³And behind the second veil, there was a tabernacle which is called the Holy of Holies, ⁴having a golden altar of incense and the ark of the covenant covered on all sides with gold, in which was a golden jar holding the manna, and Aaron's rod which budded, and the tables of the covenant. ⁵And above it were the cherubim of glory overshadowing the mercy seat; but of these things we cannot now speak in detail.

⁶Now when these things have been thus prepared, the priests are continually entering the outer tabernacle, performing the divine worship, ⁷but into the second only the high priest enters, once a year, not without taking blood, which he offers for himself and for the sins of the people committed in ignorance. ⁸The Holy Spirit is signifying this, that the way into the holy place has not yet been disclosed, while the outer tabernacle is still standing; [9]*which is a symbol for the time then present, according to which both gifts and sacrifices are offered which cannot make the worshiper perfect in conscience,* [10]*since they relate only to food and drink and various washings, regulations for the body imposed until a time of reformation.*

[11]*But when Christ appeared as a high priest of the good things to come, He entered through the greater and more perfect tabernacle, not made with hands, that is to say, not of this creation;* [12]*and not through the blood of goats and calves, but through His own blood, He entered the holy place once for all, having obtained eternal redemption.* [13]*For if the blood of goats and bulls and the ashes of a heifer sprinkling those who have been defiled, sanctify for the cleansing of the flesh,* [14]*how much more will the blood of Christ, who through the eternal Spirit offered Himself without blemish to God, cleanse your conscience from dead works to serve the living God?*

[15]*And for this reason He is the mediator of a new covenant, in order that since a death has taken place for the redemption of the transgressions that were committed under the first covenant, those who have been called may receive the promise of the eternal inheritance.*

Did you ever stop to think that members of the early Christian church never read the New Testament? For that matter, neither did the disciples. And for a very good reason. They didn't have it. Their Bible was the *Old* Testament.

When Jesus sat down with His leadership team following His resurrection to teach them what scripture actually said about Him, it was the Old Testament from which He taught. When, on the road to Emmaus, Jesus listened to two of His disciples talking of the tragedy of recent happenings, He replied to them by assuring them these events were not tragedies. Nor had they caught God off guard. Rather, they were things foretold in scripture. "And beginning with Moses and with all the prophets, He explained to them the things concerning Himself in all the Scriptures" (Luke 24:27).

Later, when the two disciples had rejoined the others in Jerusalem, Jesus appeared to the eleven and gave them an all-night Bible study, during which time He taught them from all three major divisions of Old Testament scripture: ". . . The Law of Moses and the Prophets and the Psalms . . ." (Luke 24:44).

Jesus took their Bible, the Hebrew Old Testament, and ". . . opened their minds to understand the Scriptures" (Luke 24:45). He gave the Old Testament back to them as a new book with new meaning. At long last, they were able to grasp the significance of everything which had happened to Jesus and to see how it fit into God's great plan of the ages as it had been foretold in the very scriptures which they had always had with them.

It's important to keep all this in mind as you work your way through the book of Hebrews, lest you miss the importance of the Old Testament references which appear in chapter 9. A tent in the wilderness and the rituals performed there may seem pretty dry stuff until you recall data regarding them was included in those scriptures of which Jesus said, "It is these that bear witness of Me" (John 5:39). Then these antiquities suddenly excite our interest. They have something to do with Jesus!

One of the homey bits of knowledge my father passed on to me was a saying which read: "Never take the fence down till you know why it was put up." Applied to the passage before us, this maxim suggests to me that an understanding of the Old Testament scheme will help us realize why, at long last, the good Lord put it aside. So, with this purpose in mind, let's continue our study.

From the scene and substance of Christ's ministry in chapter 8, our writer moves on to deal with the sacrificial nature and sufficiency of Christ's ministry. He draws these conclusions: *Jesus is all you need. He is the indispensable person.* So, appropriate the power available to you through Him. Achieve your full potentiality in Him. Go on from victory to victory.

One of our author's helpful literary devices is his habit of giving us a key to unlock puzzling passages. In chapter 9, we have a case in point. Two verses clarify what he is driving at in this rather lengthy parenthesis (7:1—10:18). "For if the blood of goats and bulls and the ashes of a heifer sprinkling those who have been defiled, sanctify for the cleansing of the flesh, how much more will the blood of Christ, who through the eternal Spirit offered Himself without blemish to God, cleanse your conscience from dead works to serve the living God?" (9:13,14).

If I were to give this chapter a subtitle, it might well be: "How to Handle a Nagging Conscience." There's a good deal of misunderstanding about the functions of conscience. It has been called, "a little red light in the soul." Or, as one youngster put it, "something inside which feels bad when everything else feels good."

Conscience is that internal voice which monitors your attitudes and actions. It does not determine what is right or wrong. That is established by *training*. But once you know what is right or wrong, your conscience assesses the quality of a given attitude or action, gives its verdict and then goads you into doing what you think is right and avoiding that which is wrong. However, conscience has no power to determine the outcome. That is decided by your will.

Conscience can become warped. When that happens, it is a faulty guide. The Bible reveals several kinds of out-of-kilter consciences. Jonah had a dull conscience. Jacob, an elastic conscience. Pilate, a weak conscience. Saul of Tarsus, a misguided conscience. It is not always safe or sufficient to live by your conscience. It requires training.

A marksman will hit his target only if the two sights of his rifle are correctly aligned with the bull's-eye. Similarly, your conscience gives a correct verdict only when it is correctly aligned to and trained by the living and written word of God.

Now, for the Jewish Christians to whom this book of Hebrews was written, the problem was not a conscience troubled with guilt spawned by wrongdoing. The nagging conscience plaguing them was one which needed to be purified from "dead works" (9:14). Barclay provides a bit of historical background which clarifies what I mean. "In the very earliest days, church and temple, so to speak, coexisted. We find Peter and John on their way to the temple at the hour of prayer as the most natural thing in the world. We read of them preaching in the temple courts as the obvious place in which to preach (Acts 3:1). At first there was no reason why a man should stop going to the temple just because he had begun going to church. So there was an age of transition in Jerusalem.

"But, bit by bit, something began to emerge," explains William Barclay. "It began to be clear that devotion to the temple ritual was not an innocent extra. It was something which obscured the true meaning of Christianity. A religion of grace cannot be a religion of sacrifice; a religion based on the triumphant adequacy of Jesus Christ cannot have additions to Him and to His sacrifice. And so there came a time when there had to be a clean break."[1]

Try to imagine the quandary of these Hebrew Christians. The temple had been laid out by God. The Old Testament law had been written by God. The sacrifices had been prescribed by God. Were they to turn their backs on the only God-given religion on earth and surrender themselves lock, stock and barrel to One whom their leaders called an imposter?

By throwing their traditions overboard, weren't they giving up more than they gained? If those ceremonial cleansings and ritual sacrifices had value in the past, didn't they still have merit? And, if they stopped doing all these worthwhile things, how were they to handle the problem of a nagging conscience plagued with guilt over good deeds left undone? They were really between a rock and a hard place!

Some of them solved the problem by what we might call the old-time religion approach: What was good enough for Pappy is good enough for me. Goaded by sub-Christian guilt over supposed sins of omission—the good deeds of ritual cleansing and sacrifice left undone—these fledgling followers of Jesus shifted into a high gear program of religious activity designed to make certain they pleased God and were acceptable to Him.

We may smile at their naivete, but is there any perceptible difference in motivation between their ritual washings, dietary precautions and what have you, and the equally misguided contemporary Christian's continual round of ceaseless activity designed to help gain a sense of acceptance before God? None at all. Christ plus anything equals heresy! Though we have a lot of learning and growing to do after our salvation experience, nothing can add to what Jesus has done as a means of salvation. Jesus-plus just isn't possible.

Yet, many twentieth-century saved sinners fall for the same old con job. Perhaps you have, too. You blow it with God in some area of your life. A short time later, Satan, who usually camps on the shoulder of most of us Jesus Folk, whispers in your ear, "You're not worthy of all God has done for you. At least, not now. After what you've just done. Or left undone. In fact, if you face the truth about yourself, you'll admit you're not acceptable to God at all. You better get busy and *do* something to square accounts. Otherwise, you'll never be sure God approves of you."

If you buy the devil's drivel, you'll set out on a feverish campaign designed to improve your situation. To rack up Brownie points with God. To strengthen your standing in His sight. For awhile, you may perform like Super Saint himself. But in the process, you'll wear yourself to a frazzle—going to meetings; serving on committees; passing out tracts; even teaching Sunday School—hoping thereby to win the affection, approval and acceptance of God. You may be doing the right things, but you will be doing them for the wrong reason. As a result, you end up frustrated. Joyless. Uncertain.

As one lady said to her pastor, "I don't know what's wrong with me. I do all I can to serve the Lord, and I still feel guilty. Then I feel guilty about feeling guilty." Precisely. It *is* discouraging to see all this laudable effort dismissed as "dead works." It's disconcerting to learn such effort, as a means of earning another spiritual merit badge, just doesn't register with God. He simply isn't impressed by feverish effort.

THE FUTILITY OF ACTIVITY

What's the answer? A secularized Christianity takes the "We're number two" approach. Believe in Jesus and try harder. That sounds deceptively pious, but it is dangerously pagan. If we listen to what the writer of Hebrews says, we will quickly recognize the utter futility of activity when it comes to getting or staying in tune with God.

"Now even the first covenant had regulations of divine worship and the earthly sanctuary. For there was a tabernacle prepared, the outer one, in which were the lampstand and the table and the sacred bread; this is called the holy place. And behind the second veil there was a tabernacle which is called the Holy of Holies, having a golden altar of incense and the ark of the covenant covered on all sides with gold, in which was a golden jar holding the manna, and Aaron's rod which budded, and the tables of the covenant.

"And above it were the cherubim of glory overshadowing the mercy seat; but of these things we cannot now speak in detail. Now when these things have been thus prepared, the priests are continually entering the outer tabernacle, performing the divine worship, but into the second only the high priest enters, once a year, not without taking blood, which he offers for himself and for the sins of the people committed in ignorance.

"The Holy Spirit is signifying this, that the way into the holy place has not yet been disclosed, while the outer tabernacle is still standing, which is a symbol for the time then present, according to which both gifts and sacrifices are offered which cannot make the worshiper perfect in conscience, since they relate only to food and drink and various washings, regulations for the body imposed until a time of reformation" (9:1-10).

The tent (tabernacle) in the wilderness was meant to be an object lesson pointing to Jesus, as shown in figure 1.[2]

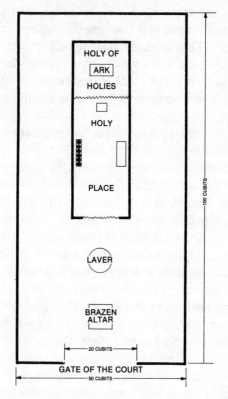

Figure 1

The tabernacle consisted of three distinct units: the outer court and two interior rooms. Inside the gate of the outer court were the brazen altar and laver. Beyond these were two tent rooms in tandem, separated by a curtain which historians variously say was four to six inches thick. The first chamber was called the Holy Place. It contained the golden candlestick on the left and the table of shewbread on the right. Immediately in front of the veil was the altar of incense. The priests regularly entered into this first section to make their daily sacrifices to God.

The most sacred area was the inner room, the Holy of Holies, beyond the separating veil. This area housed the ark of the covenant with ". . . the cherubim of glory overshadowing the mercy seat . . ." (9:5). Permeated with the glory of God, it was a place where only the high priest was permitted, and then just once a year on the day of atonement. (It is not my intention to deal with the apparent problem posed by verses 3 and 4 which mention the Holy of Holies having a golden altar of incense. Those interested in pursuing the matter will find help from several sources listed among the bibliography.)

The tabernacle was the earthly center of Jewish faith and worship. It was the one place where, more than any other, Jehovah was thought to dwell. The ark in the Holy of Holies was believed to be God's home on earth. It was always kept closed. But Jehovah could be reached if anything were placed on the lid, or mercy seat, as it was called. This was as close as human gifts could get to God. Thus, the mercy seat became the place par excellence. The spot on which atonement must be made and the dark smirch of sin erased.

A quick look at the following diagram will show that, just inside the gate, was the brazen altar where portions of the animal sacrifice were burned. At the far end was the ark of the covenant in God's throne room, the Holy of Holies. As figure 2 indicates, the God-given arrangement of these and the other pieces of furniture, all of which were beautiful pictures of some aspect of our Lord's life and person, formed the shadow of a cross.

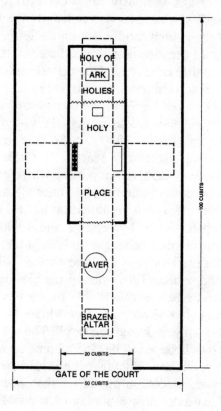

Figure 2

Undoubtedly, Jesus pointed this out to His disciples during that nightlong Bible class when He showed them how eloquently the Old Testament scriptures spoke of Him. For the tabernacle clearly spelled out how *Christians* are to approach God.

As saved sinners we must first accept Christ as our substitute (John 1:29), so we begin at the brazen altar. But Jesus can do more than save us from the penalty of sin; He can cleanse us from the power of sin. Thus, the next step is to take Jesus as our sanctifier (John 3:5), the One who washes us with the water of life, so we move to the laver.

At this point, we must permit Him to be our light and guide (John 8:12), represented by the golden candlestick. We must also feed on Him who said, ". . . I am the bread of life . . ." (John 6:35), and across the way is the table of shewbread. Because He is the One who now intercedes for us and through whom our prayers reach God (John 14:13,14; Hebrews 9:24), we must pass by the altar of incense. At this point, we reach the veil which, at one time, separated sinners from the presence of God.

But when Jesus died on the cross, the veil was torn in two (Matthew 27:51). So, we discover redeemed sinners can enter into the Holy of Holies "by a new and living way which He [Jesus] inaugurated for us through the veil, that is, His flesh" (Hebrews 10:20). The whole tabernacle speaks of Christ in many ways. Not the least of these is that over and through it all is the shadow of the cross (figure 2).

It's difficult for us contemporary Christians to understand the sanctity of this place in the thoughts and emotions of the ancient Jews. The tabernacle was super special. The music, pageantry, color and ritual of the old sacrificial system undoubtedly held a spell over some of the early Hebrew Christians. And quite understandably so. Its services must have been moving and memorable.

A little girl was walking with her daddy one night. The stars above were like diamonds stuck in the black ore of space. As she gazed up at the splendor of the sky, she suddenly exclaimed, "Oh, Daddy, if the wrong side of

91

heaven is so beautiful, what must the right side be like!"

That's precisely the point our author is making. He lovingly remembers the awe-inspiring beauty of the tabernacle and seems to say, "If this *earthly* place and form of worship were so beautiful and moving, what must the *true* sanctuary and worship in heaven be like!" He sees the Old Testament layout and ritual as symbolic. A beautiful object lesson of the better way Jesus had introduced. Because, for all their splendor, the Old Testament provisions had no power in themselves. They could not remove sin. They could not cleanse the conscience. They could not instigate full and free fellowship between God and man.

The old system dramatized its own inadequacy. An atonement which needed to be repeated over and over could not provide assurance one's sin was gone. A conscience needing to be cleansed again and again, year in and year out, had not really been cleansed at all. Under the old system, ". . . the priests are *continually* entering the outer tabernacle . . ." (9:6). Under these circumstances, sin and guilt, which plague the conscience like weeds, were being chopped off at ground level. The roots, which remained, burrowed deeper and each spring new growth sprouted. Though the old system had strong external visual value, it did not reach the root of the problem. It did not deal a deathblow to sin.

Nor did it make possible full and free access to God. That's the symbolism of the two rooms divided by the veil, behind which the high priest alone could go, and then just once a year. As long as this holy place remained inaccessible, the Holy Spirit was saying, ". . . the way into the holy place [the very presence of God] has not yet been disclosed . . ." (9:8).

The insufficiency of the old system was evident. The daily stream of priests going in and out of the main part of the tabernacle—tending the lamp, renewing the incense and, every seven days, changing the bread—were dramatic proof that, despite the richness of this ritual, the daily and annual ministrations did little good. They only affected the outer man. They were "regulations for the body" (9:10). They could not perfect the conscience (9:9). They did not touch the inner man.

The old system was bankrupt. And, the moment Jesus died, the entire Old Testament religious system ceased to have any meaning to man or standing with God. At long last, the real thing had come. The Old Testament sacrificial system had served its purpose. I am sure we shall meet many Old Testament people in heaven. Nevertheless, the Old Testament sacrifices were incomplete, involuntary and at long last, they became unnecessary.

So, God abolished the first in order to establish the second. As long as those first-century Hebrew Christians remembered, believed, and lived by that, they were free. They were able to handle the problem of recurring sin in a creative way. They called it by its rightful name: sin! They confessed it to God. Repented. Were forgiven. Got back on the track of letting Jesus live His life through them.

But when, as sinner-saints, they began to question their acceptability to God—when they began to believe various forms of religious activity could add something to what Jesus had done for them on the cross; or, believing there was real value in mere ritual and realizing they were not fulfilling that ritual, were goaded by a nagging conscience into an endless routine of dead works—the joy of the Lord vanished. And they fell prey to the acme of futility: pointless, ceaseless, religious activity, all of which was powerless to affect their relationship to God.

What was true of them is true of you and me. Your relationship to God does not depend on what you do for God, but what God in Christ has done for you. He doesn't love you one whit more because you wear yourself to a nub serving Him. God loves you because God is love and it is the nature of love to be loving!

You do not make yourself any more acceptable to Him because you commit yourself to some high-powered program of Bible study, witnessing, or social action. You are acceptable to God because He sees you through Christ. Christ is perfect. Therefore, you are perfect from God's perspective. You are acceptable to Him—He approves of you— because when He looks at you all He sees is Jesus. The key word is "all." He doesn't see your sin. He sees Jesus. He doesn't see your frantic antics to make yourself more lovable and acceptable. He sees Jesus. That's *all* He sees, but that's enough!

"For by grace [God's Riches At Christ's Expense] you have been saved through faith [plus nothing]; and that not of yourselves [not your own doing], it is the gift of God; not as a result of works, that no one should boast" (Ephesians 2:8,9). Once this truth hits home, you will be free. You will realize the utter futility of ceaseless activity aimed, even subconsciously, at improving your relationship to God.

THE ADEQUACY OF REALITY

In contrast to the futility of activity as a means of salvation, the writer of Hebrews focuses our attention on the adequacy of reality. "But when Christ appeared as a high priest of the good things to come, He entered through the greater and more perfect tabernacle not made with hands, that is to say, not of this creation; and not through the blood of goats and calves but through His own blood, He entered the holy place once for all, having obtained eternal redemption.

"For if the blood of goats and bulls and the ashes of a

heifer sprinkling those who have been defiled, sanctify for the cleansing of the flesh, how much more will the blood of Christ, who through the eternal Spirit offered Himself without blemish to God, cleanse your conscience from dead works to serve the living God?'' (9:11-14).

When our author refers to Christ as "a high priest of the good things to come" (9:11), he introduces us to the adequacy of reality. (Although the New American Standard Bible shows this as "to come," they footnote that some ancient manuscripts read, "that have come.") This is not something which will happen to us some day in the sweet by-and-by. Jesus *is* what's happening! His ministry on our behalf is related to the everyday needs of *now*. He is the "high priest of the good things to [that have] come."

Among these contemporary "good things" is the knowledge that "the blood of Jesus His Son cleanses us from all sin" (I John 1:7b). The real futility of pointless religious activity is that it cannot solve our problem. It cannot touch the inner man. It can only give us a kind of surface glaze which may dazzle others as they see us rush through our days, but which leaves us empty.

God wants to work and dwell in us at the deepest level. In that "Holy of Holies" which is our own spirit. Figure 1 illustrates my meaning. Our body is symbolized by the outer court. Our soul by the holy place. Our spirit by the Holy of Holies. It is there, and only there, we can really commune with God. Jesus said, "God is spirit, and those who worship Him must worship in spirit and truth" (John 4:24). But the problem lay in the fact that the very place God wanted to work and dwell in was inaccessible to Him.

Figure 3 illustrates man's state before and after the fall (Genesis 1—3). Man, as originally designed, was linked to the triune God by a spiritual hot line through which

God's Holy Spirit indwelt man's human spirit and communicated with him. When ego exerted itself, sin resulted and the linkage between God and man was broken.

Until Jesus came and offered Himself without blemish to God (9:14), all men were ". . . dead in [their]

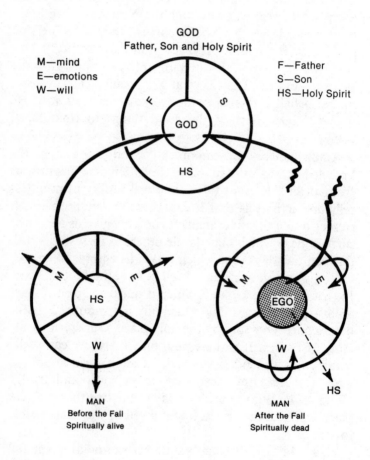

Figure 3

trespasses and sins'' (Ephesians 2:1). There was no way God could work and dwell with the human race at the deepest level. He had to limit Himself to surface solutions. But when Jesus came and, through His cross, opened a way into this area (figure 4), it was possible, for the

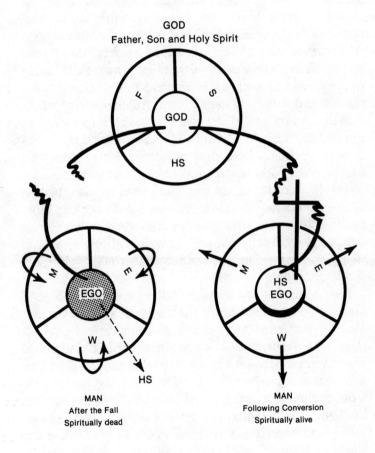

Figure 4

first time since the fall, for man to be spiritually alive.

God's Holy Spirit dwelt in the human spirit again. Born-again men became complete human beings as their spirits began to function. Alive in the truest sense. Functioning as God intended men to function. All of this, our writer says, is accomplished by the blood of Christ (9:14).

What is it about Christ's blood which makes it unique? To answer that question, we examine figure 3 again. As God first made him, man was a tripartite being—consisting of body, soul and spirit. At the control center—or, to continue our present figure of speech, the throne room, the Holy of Holies—dwelt God's own Holy Spirit. (Note circle to lower left in figure 3.) With God's Spirit feeding and fortifying man's spirit, Adam was truly alive.

When Adam sinned, he died spiritually. (Note circle to lower right in figure 3.) God's Holy Spirit left him. (Coincidentally, Adam later died physically as an aftereffect of his earlier spiritual death.) Now, the reason Adam could die because of sin was that, prior to his rebellion against God, he was alive; he was filled with the Holy Spirit. Those of us who have come after Adam have never been alive spiritually until Christ moves in to give us life. Being sons of Adam, at birth we inherit his spiritually dead condition.

But, Jesus was not a son of Adam; He was the Son of God. Jesus has been called the "second Adam" because He was patterned after the first Adam *before* the fall (figure 5). Jesus could die for sin and His blood could atone for sin because He *was the only man since Adam who was really alive;* that is, filled with the Holy Spirit from the moment of physical birth and throughout His lifetime. That's what the Bible means when it says, ". . . God [the Holy Spirit] was in Christ reconciling the world to Himself . . ." (II Corinthians 5:19).

In the strictest sense of the word, in all history there

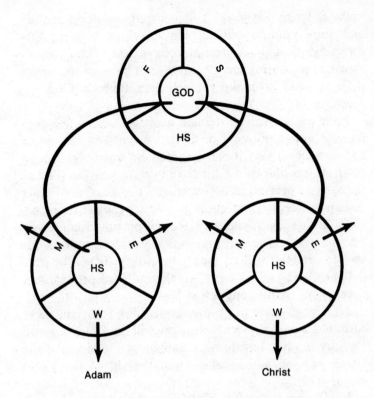

Figure 5

have been only two deaths because of sin. Death occurred once in Adam because of his disobedience. It occurred a second time in Jesus because of His obedience unto death. Because Christ's death was adequate, it will never be repeated. When you become a Christian, your spirit is quickened. The Holy Spirit of God occupies your "Holy of Holies." You are made alive. Really alive. Everlastingly alive. That's what Jesus meant when He said, "I came that they might have life" (John 10:10b).

All this is accomplished through the blood of Christ. There's nothing you can add to what Jesus has done to

99

make it more complete. Tell yourself this long enough and loud enough until it hardens into a firm, life-directing, thought-controlling conviction. Then Satan's effort at generating sub-Christian guilt because you aren't doing enough to make yourself acceptable to God will fail.

Your conscience will remain quiet because, when confronted with the blood of Christ, a nagging conscience has nothing to say! It is left speechless when you remind yourself the blood of Christ completely satisfies God as far as your perfection is concerned. The heavenly Father does not accept you because you wear yourself to a frazzle in futile religious activity. He accepts you because you are in Christ. When you grasp that wonderful fact, your service for Him will no longer be a duty. It will be pure delight. A way of saying: "Thank you, Jesus; thank you, thank you, thank you, Jesus!"

And forgiveness will not be something you struggle to earn as a saved sinner. Instead, it will be a blessing you joyfully receive, having been bought by the blood of the Lamb of God which takes away the sin of the world (John 1:29).

Joe Blinco, a gentle spiritual giant now gone to be with God, was often heard to say, "A thousand times I've failed Christ. A thousand times I've forfeited my right to heaven. A thousand times I've marred the image of God in me. But ten thousand times ten thousand Christ has been ready, willing and able to forgive me. Cleanse me. Point me in the right direction again. And use me." That's grace. The unmerited, undeserved, unearned goodness of God made possible through the blood of Christ.

Joe Blinco didn't focus on his failure, but upon God's success. That's something all saved sinners must learn to do. During the heat of temptation it helps to talk to Satan about the blood of Christ. Such talk puts you on the offensive, and him on the defensive. The rest of the time you should remind yourself of the precious, healing stream which flows from Calvary. Repeatedly you should remind yourself of what Jesus has done.

What you say to yourself is important. If you believe the devil's lies that you're worthless, hopeless and useless, you will be goaded by an uneasy conscience into trying to make yourself acceptable to God through "dead works." If you remind yourself that the blood of Christ completely satisfies God as far as you are concerned, the pressure will be off for you to do anything to make yourself more safe and secure.

The burden of adequacy will no longer be on your back, because one day it was placed on His back in the form of a cross. What had to be done, Jesus did. Now, because He lives to make intercession for you—because Jesus *is* what's happening—He is doing and will continue to do what needs to be done in, to and through you.

6

OUR HOPE: Jesus Is What's Happening

Hebrews 9:16—10:18

FOR where a covenant is, there must of necessity be the death of the one who made it. [17]For a covenant is valid only when men are dead, for it is never in force while the one who made it lives. [18]Therefore even the first covenant was not inaugurated without blood. [19]For when every commandment had been spoken by Moses to all the people according to the Law, he took the blood of the calves and the goats, with water and scarlet wool and hyssop, and sprinkled both the book itself and all the people, [20]saying, "This is the blood of the covenant which God commanded you." [21]And in the same way he sprinkled both the tabernacle and all the vessels of the ministry with the blood. [22]And according to the Law, one may almost say, all things are cleansed with blood, and without shedding of blood there is no forgiveness.

[23]Therefore it was necessary for the copies of the things in the heavens to be cleansed with these, but the heavenly things themselves with better sacrifices than these. [24]For Christ did not enter a holy place made with hands, a mere copy of the true one, but into heaven itself, now to appear in

the presence of God for us; [25]nor was it that He should offer Himself often, as the high priest enters the holy place year by year with blood not his own. [26]Otherwise, He would have needed to suffer often since the foundation of the world; but now once at the consummation He has been manifested to put away sin by the sacrifice of Himself.

[27]And inasmuch as it is appointed for men to die once, and after this comes judgment; [28]so Christ also, having been offered once to bear the sins of many, shall appear a second time, not to bear sin, to those who eagerly await Him, for salvation.

For the Law, since it has only a shadow of the good things to come and not the very form of things, can never by the same sacrifices year by year, which they offer continually, make perfect those who draw near. [2]Otherwise, would they not have ceased to be offered, because the worshipers, having once been cleansed, would no longer have had consciousness of sins? [3]But in those sacrifices there is a reminder of sins year by year. [4]For it is impossible for the blood of bulls and goats to take away sins. [5]Therefore, when He comes into the world, He says,

"Sacrifice and offering Thou has not desired,
But a body Thou hast prepared for Me;
[6]In whole burnt offerings and sacrifices for sin
Thou hast taken no pleasure.
[7]"Then I said, 'Behold, I have come
(In the roll of the book it is written of Me)
To do Thy will, O God.' "
[8]After saying above, "Sacrifices and offerings and whole burnt offerings and sacrifices for sin Thou hast not desired, nor hast Thou taken pleasure in them" (which are offered according to the Law), [9]then He said, "Behold, I have come to do Thy will." He takes away the first in order to

establish the second. [10]*By this will we have been sanctified through the offering of the body of Jesus Christ once for all.*

[11]*And every priest stands daily ministering and offering time after time the same sacrifices, which can never take away sins;* [12]*but He, having offered one sacrifice for sins for all time, sat down at the right hand of God,* [13]*waiting from that time onward until His enemies be made a footstool for His feet.* [14]*For by one offering He has perfected for all time those who are sanctified.*

[15]*And the Holy Spirit also bears witness to us; for after saying,*

> [16]*"This is the covenant that I will make with them*
> *After those days, says the Lord:*
> *I will put My laws upon their heart,*
> *And upon their mind I will write them,"*

He then says,

> [17]*"And their sins and their lawless deeds*
> *I will remember no more."*

[18]*Now where there is forgiveness of these things, there is no longer any offering for sin.*

Structurally speaking, the first eighteen verses of chapter 10 are a reiteration, with additional scriptural references, of everything the writer has said in chapters 8 and 9. As such, these eighteen verses do not require separate exegesis. However, they round out our grasp of Christ's action on our behalf. "For the Law since it has only a shadow of the good things to come and not the very form of things, can never by the same sacrifices year by year which they offer continually, make perfect those who draw near. Otherwise, would they not have ceased to be offered, because the worshipers, having once been cleansed, would no longer have had consciousness of sins?" (10:1,2).

Usually the New American Standard Bible is more correct and clear than our cherished King James Version. In this case, the opposite is true. At the end of verse 2, the New American asks the question, if the law were effective in getting through to God, wouldn't the cleansed person "no longer have had consciousness of sin?" If the NAS is correct, the inference is that Christians who *do* get through to God no longer have any consciousness of sins.

Our author's argument throughout has been that under the old system, that is, Judaism, worshipers did *not* get through to God. They were, thus, plagued by a continuing consciousness of sins which denied them rest. But we all know from experience that, following cleansing, our consciousness of sins is often sharpened. Attitudes and actions we were once able to tolerate in ourselves are now unacceptable. In fact, the closer we get to Jesus, the greater our consciousness of sins.

The King James Version says worshipers who really get through to God "have had no more conscience of sins." This, in my judgment, is the correct translation. The word conscience appears over 30 times in the New Testament. Each time the same Greek word is used: *suneidesis.* This is the word used by our author. It means more than mere intellectual knowledge or awareness. It involves the emotional life as well. It has to do with feelings of goodness or guilt.

The thing Jesus does, which that old system could not do, is cleanse the conscience—the thinking, feeling center of our being. Once a sinner has turned from waywardness and committed himself to God in Christ, moral innocence is restored. The man in Christ has only Christ's past which is perfect. Wholly acceptable to God. Therefore, while he may have a *consciousness* of sinning, there is, through confession and repentance, a cleansing of his *conscience.* The guilt may be remembered intellectually, but the sting of guilt is gone emotionally. The forgiven man knows he has sinned, but he no longer feels it.[1]

Each time we come to God with the problem of recurring sin, as we saved sinners surely must—confess it, repent of it, claim forgiveness for it—we are given more of Christ's perfect past. And so it goes. Moment by moment. Day by day. Week by week. Year by year. As long as life lasts. The good Lord continues to give us more and more of Christ's past until at long last, when we are absent from the body and at home with Him, we present to Him a slate which has been made clean by the blood of the Lamb.

The picture most helpful to me in this regard is that of a field of new blown snow stretching as far as the eye can see—and beyond! Freshness and whiteness are everywhere. The landscape is cloaked in purity. That's a portrait of our past in Christ. It is spotless, from each moment of confession and repentance back into the eternity of God. "If we confess our sins, He is faithful and righteous to forgive us our sins and to cleanse us from all unrighteousness" (I John 1:9).

Note this incredible truth: God cleanses us of *all* unrighteousness! Not just the sins we confess, but the sins we do not confess because we aren't yet convicted of their sinfulness. There are things in my life I do not yet recognize as sin. Others may see them. My wife does (or so she insists)! I don't. The Holy Spirit has not yet revealed these chinks in my Christian character to me. Thus, I can't honestly confess them to God.

But the Lord knows the debilitating effect of unconfessed sin in a Christian's life. Therefore, when I confess those sins of which I am conscious, God in His goodness cleanses me of *all* unrighteousness, including those things I do not yet recognize as sin. In that moment of God-washed-cleanness, I stand before Him spotless, with no past but the past of Christ which is perfect. Hallelujah!

Does that mean past sins are forgotten? From God's perspective, yes. From ours, no. We would all like to forget some of our sins, as well as some of those committed against us. But, to hope for that is to hope for something which cannot be. It is impossible. This brain of ours is a physical computer with a memory bank which cannot forget. A psychologist told me recently of new forms of treatment used to quicken areas of memory which were thought to be lost. Under prodding, however, memory was discovered to be still there.

Hoping to forget our sinful past is unrealistic. But, we *can* put a new meaning on our memory. It can serve to remind us of areas of danger we need to avoid because of past susceptibility. Memory can serve to remind us of the amazing grace of God and of those things of which He in His love has cleansed us. We still know we've sinned, but that knowledge does not plague us. To the contrary, it is a cause for rejoicing, for we also know, with even greater certainty, that we have been forgiven!

Jesus people are not spared from a *consciousness* of sins, but we no longer have a *conscience* of sin. Though we fail our heavenly Father, we can return to Him with absolute confidence, knowing the blood of Jesus Christ cleanses us from all unrighteousness (I John 1:9). Thus, our conscience no longer sears us with burning regret over a past which God has completely cleansed and forgiven.

When you get that message loud and clear, you will no longer feel any compulsion to become involved in a feverish, ceaseless round of religious activity aimed at making yourself more acceptable to God. Christianity is not some feeble effort on your part to live a shoddy imitation of Jesus. Christianity is Jesus living His life in you here and now. Right where you are. Through your set of genes, chromosomes and glands. In your set of circumstances.

In his first letter to the Corinthians, the Apostle Paul says, "Do you not know that you are a temple of God, and that the Spirit of God dwells in you?" (I Corinthians 3:16). That ancient tent-tabernacle in the wilderness is gone. So, too, is the beautiful temple in Jerusalem. But *the* temple, the Christian believer's life, is more in evidence today than ever before. And, of course, that has been God's game plan from the very beginning. God has not been primarily concerned with getting men to heaven, though that's important to Him. His primary concern has been to find a way to get Himself back into man on earth. When we are "born again" (John 3:3), God's purpose becomes possible. He is given a body through which to function. Your body. And mine.

That's one of the amazing truths of the Christian faith. God's tabernacle, or dwelling place today, is in the Christian believer. If you are a Christian, the Lord Jesus clothes Himself in your personality and lives His life over again in your circumstances. In the process, you experience the adequacy of reality.

All the Father was to Jesus, Jesus is to you! As a Christian you are plugged into a source of spiritual supply which never runs dry. Your dependence is not upon "dead works" (9:14), but upon the free flowing power of the living Christ who dwells in you. Jesus *is* what's happening. In heaven, yes. But also in your heart, right here on earth. ". . . You are a temple of God, and . . . the Spirit of God dwells in you" (I Corinthians 3:16).

Have you been slow to grasp this precious truth? Have you been quick to rush back to legalism and reject your liberty in Christ? Have you been an easy prey for Satan's foil whereby he attempts to get you feverishly locked up in the futility of activity, trying to make yourself more acceptable to God? If so, write this down in living letters of fire upon your memory: *Christ's death completely satisfies God as far as your perfection is concerned.* The blood of Jesus Christ is adequate. There is no adding to it. No mixing with it. No going beyond it. It is complete. Satisfactory. Final. Thus, you can reject the futility of activity as a means of grace and rest in the adequacy of reality.

THE EFFICACY OF FINALITY

The last thread in our author's argument is the efficacy of finality. We see it in chapter 9, verses 11 through 28, describing the ministry of the high priest as he applies the blood of the sacrifice in the tabernacle rituals. Our author shows that when Christ appeared as our high priest He applied His own blood once for all in the holy place of the greater and more perfect tabernacle—one not made with hands—and thereby obtained our eternal redemption.

Among other things, efficacy involves power to perform. That old hymn, "There Is Power in the Blood," comes to mind:

> Would you be free from the burden of sin?
> There's power in the blood.
> Would you o'er evil a victory win?
> There's wonderful power in the blood.

Many recoil at this coupling of blood with the Christian faith. Lucille, my wife, tells of a college dorm mate who, when the blood of Christ was mentioned, said, "Ohhhhh, that sounds messy." Others speak caustically of Christianity as a "slaughterhouse religion." Their very words reveal their utter insensitivity to and abysmal ignorance of the scarlet thread which runs through scripture.

Just *why* blood is indispensable to the forgiveness of sin is a secret locked in the mind of God. But, surely, the repeated sacrifice of substitutionary animals, leading finally to the shed blood of Jesus, clearly fixes the fact that forgiveness is a costly thing. It's no "tsk, tsk" matter. It involves brokenness.

Blood is a mysterious fluid intimately associated with life. We moderns who know so much about chemistry can easily lose the awe once felt by those who believed life is in the blood (Leviticus 17:11). For them to give God blood was to give God life—the highest and best of all gifts. When we turn that truth around and remember, ". . . God was in Christ [on that cross] reconciling [us] to

Himself" (II Corinthians 5:19), we begin to see that in the blood of Jesus, God was offering *us* the best of *His* gifts. And, we begin to understand the true meaning of love.

One of our college students stopped by just now with what he termed a mind-blower. "I've been thinking about the meaning of love," he said. "I've come to realize love says 'I die for you.' Not, 'I will die for you'. Nor 'I would, if necessary, die for you'. But 'I do die for you'. In other words," he went on, "love says to the loved one, 'From my perspective, you're more important than I am. I put your joy, fulfillment and self-realization ahead of my own.' "

Well, as my young friend said, that is a mind-blower. For the Bible declares: "God is love" (I John 4:8). Love says, "I die for you." And God, who is love, did just that! When God in Christ was nailed to a cross, in effect, He was saying, "Man, from My perspective you're more important than I am. I lay down My life for you. I put your joy, fulfillment and self-realization ahead of My own. I die for you." When that wonderful truth penetrates, we concur with Isaac Watts: "Love so amazing, so divine, Demands my soul, my life, my all."

We begin to understand and to say, "Oh, no, God, that's all wrong! *You're* more important than I am, I die for *You.*" Thus, we stop sinning. That is, we stop trying to be our own God. We put Him first. Willingly. Joyfully. Increasingly. We say, "God, I die for You." And, in the process of losing our life, we find it—just as Jesus promised (Matthew 10:39). God's loving desire for us is accomplished. We are reborn. Made whole. Liberated from the ego which would rule us. And our joy is complete—for both the Redeemer and the redeemed.

Christ's sacrifice was retroactive. He settled accounts for all who acted in faith under the terms of the old contract. The new covenant is greater than the old. The greater includes the lesser. Therefore, those Jews who were promised an inheritance (9:15), received it through Christ. Their faithfulness to the light they had, met the qualification of salvation "by grace . . . through faith" (Ephesians 2:8).

To further fix the indispensability of Christ's blood in our heart, our author uses the illustration of a will (covenant). "For where a covenant [will] is, there must of necessity be the death of the one who made it. For a covenant is valid only when men are dead, for it is never in force while the one who made it lives" (9:16,17).

His logic is clear. The benefits of a will only come to the beneficiaries after the death of the benefactor. The last will and testament of our Lord Jesus Christ, the new covenant, included many riches. For us to inherit these, it was necessary for Jesus to die. The shedding of Christ's blood put the will into effect.

But sometimes a will can be broken. The desires of the deceased are violated. So the writer of Hebrews announces some incredible news: Jesus is what's happening! He not only died to activate His will, He made Himself executor of that new covenant. Because of His resurrection, He now lives to intercede for us. To guarantee that our adversary, the devil, will never succeed in breaking the terms of Christ's will.

That's what it means to have Jesus as our intercessor. He isn't trying to convince God to be kind and loving, as if God were otherwise. Nor is he attempting to get God to forgive us, as if God were unwilling to do so. Everything the Son does, He does on behalf of and in concert with the Father. As our intercessor, Jesus is bringing to bear upon our situation all the resources of heaven so Satan will never succeed in breaking the conditions of His will.

We often speak of the finished work of Christ, and we thank God for the fact that Jesus died "once for all"

(9:26,28), and later "sat down at the right hand of God" (10:12) to dramatize the efficacy and finality of His all-sufficient sacrifice. In the Old Testament tabernacle, there were no chairs. Instead, day after day, year after year, century after century, the priests bustled about the tabernacle—coming and going—in the never-ending business of making sacrifices for sin. But when Christ had offered for all time a single sacrifice for sin, He sat down (10:12). His job was over. So, we thank God for the finished work of Christ. It gives us a great sense of security and serenity.

But we should also be grateful for the unfinished work of Christ. His ministry of intercession. "For Christ did not enter a holy place made with hands, a mere copy of the true one, but into heaven itself, now to appear in the presence of God for us" (9:24).

His sacrifice on earth was once for all. His intercessory ministry in heaven is perpetual. Through the first, we are put into relationship with God. Through the second, we are kept in fellowship with God. Our relationship is final and complete. Our fellowship must be renewed and refreshed day by day.

Someone has said, "Sin twines through my thoughts and slips into my prayers." With each intrusion of sin, Satan, our adversary, tries to create a cleavage in our fellowship with God. But Christ, our high priest, steps in to intercede for us. To remind us His sacrifice covers all our sin—past, present and future—so there need never be even a moment's break in our fellowship with the heavenly Father. This special intercessory ministry of Christ will never end as long as a solitary sinner-saint is in the place of testing here on earth. As long as one of us is under siege by Satan, the intercessory ministry of Jesus will be working on our behalf to keep us creative and free.

Thank God for the unfinished work of Christ. Jesus

is what's happening! Now. Today. In heaven and in your heart. He is active at this very moment on your behalf, administering the conditions of a will He died to activate. A will in which you inherit forgiveness of sin. A cleansed conscience. Victory in time. Hope in eternity. The blessed assurance of immediate access to God any moment of the night or day.

While this is really too wonderful for words, the best is yet to be. Christ ". . . shall appear a second time, not to bear sin, but to those who eagerly await Him . . ." (9:28). Here the Hebrew day of atonement is in our author's mind. He is thinking of the high priest who would take off his beautiful garments of glory and, clothed in a robe of white linen, go into the Holy of Holies to perform his tasks.

While the high priest was in the Holy of Holies, there was great anxiety among the people outside. It was a time of tense waiting. He had gone into the very presence of God on their behalf. To offer God their prayers of confession and repentance. Would these be acceptable? The reappearance of the high priest, now dressed in his royal robes, was an especially welcome sight. It meant God had approved of their sacrifice. He had forgiven their sins.

With all of this in mind, the writer of Hebrews thinks of Jesus, the Christian's high priest, Who took off His garments of heavenly glory and, clothed in the white linen of spotless manhood, set out to make atonement for sin. This completed, He entered the heavenly sanctuary where He now intercedes for us. We need not worry or wonder if God will accept His sacrifice. Or hear His prayers of intercession. The resurrection is proof of that. It is God's seal of acceptance on all Jesus was and did. His sacrifice was enough.

But one day He shall return in robes of regal glory. Not to deal with sin. He has already done that. But, to bring final and total fulfillment to those "who are (eagerly, constantly and patiently) waiting and expecting him" (9:28, Amplified Bible). Little wonder Philip Bliss wrote in the hymn "Hallelujah, What a Saviour," "Man of sorrows, what a name, for the Son of God who came, ruined sinners to reclaim. Hallelujah! What a Saviour!"

7

HIS SECOND COMING: Your Joy or Judgment

Hebrews 10:26-39

FOR if we go on sinning willfully after receiving the knowledge of the truth, there no longer remains a sacrifice for sins, ²⁷but a certain terrifying expectation of judgment, and the fury of a fire which will consume the adversaries. ²⁸Anyone who has set aside the Law of Moses dies without mercy on the testimony of two or three witnesses.

²⁹How much severer punishment do you think he will deserve who has trampled under foot the Son of God, and has regarded as unclean the blood of the covenant by which he was sanctified, and has insulted the Spirit of grace? ³⁰For we know Him who said, "Vengeance is Mine, I will repay." And again, "The Lord will judge His people." ³¹It is a terrifying thing to fall into the hands of the living God.

³²But remember the former days, when, after being enlightened, you endured a great conflict of sufferings, ³³partly, by being made a public spectacle through reproaches and tribulations, and partly by becoming sharers with those who were so treated. ³⁴For you showed sympathy to the prisoners, and accepted joyfully the seizure of your property, knowing that you have for yourselves a better possession and an abiding one. ³⁵Therefore, do not throw away your confidence, which has a great reward. ³⁶For you have need of endurance, so that when you have done the will of God, you may receive what was promised.

³⁷For yet in a very little while,
He who is coming will come, and will not delay.
³⁸But My righteous one shall live by faith;
And if he shrinks back, My soul has no pleasure in him.
³⁹But we are not of those who shrink back to destruction, but of those who have faith to the preserving of the soul.

We come now to the beginning of the end of Hebrews. Our author's monumental arguments for the superiority, supremacy and sufficiency of Christ are over. Because he is a seasoned teacher and recognizes the short-term nature of the average person's memory span, he will yet reinforce his argument with a few additional references to who Jesus was and what Jesus did, but, for the most part, his courtly comment on the unexcelled excellence of Christ is completed. Now he focuses our attention upon the everyday implications of this. His theme from here on out will be: the urgency of practicality.

A sensitive pastor, he will not neglect the "So what?" element in his teaching. He refuses to deal with doctrine in isolation from daily living. This has been characteristic of his style throughout. Instead of using a straight-line method of reasoning, he has followed a somewhat serpentine course. Interweaving the practical with the theoretical. Never failing to wed the two. On occasion, he has lifted us into the stratosphere of the Spirit with some soaring statement about the Saviour. But, before we become too other-worldly in our thinking, he has suddenly jerked us back to earth with a stunning rebuke or loving exhortation.

Along with being a seasoned teacher and a sensitive pastor, he is also a sound psychologist. To insure that his words of warning have maximum impact, he uses an adaptation of the sandwich technique: compliment, correction, compliment. You will see this develop as we move along.

The opening sentence in his summation (10:19-25) blends together the three great Christian virtues of faith, hope and love. "Since therefore, brethren, we have confidence to enter the holy place by the blood of Jesus, by a new and living way which He inaugurated for us through the veil, that is, His flesh, and since we have a great priest over the house of God, let us draw near with a sincere heart in full assurance of faith, having our hearts sprinkled clean from an evil conscience and our body washed with pure water" (10:19-22).

According to the writer of Hebrews, faith is confidence to enter. To enter what? The Holy of Holies within our being; that is, our once dead spirit which has been quickened by Christ and where God through Christ chooses to meet us. "Do you not know that you are a temple of God and that the Spirit of God dwells in you?" (I Corinthians 3:16).

Faith perceives the incredible fact that God and the child of God are no longer two distinct persons. Through Christ, you and He are one. God has become a part of your life as a Christian. You have become a part of God's life and action in life. The veil has been torn in two. There is nothing between. The implications of this in terms of daily living are staggering.

Many saved sinners act as if the veil were still in place. They still think of God as a vague, oblong blur. A distant Being out there somewhere in space. As a result, they're lonely. Frustrated. Guilt-ridden. Despairing. They have no conception of the liberty and security which is theirs in Christ. They still think of themselves as people on probation who, if they work long enough and hard enough, will finally make themselves fit enough for fellowship with God. What they fail to realize is that their acceptability to

Him and His accessibility to them does not depend upon any noble, but futile, effort of their own. The Christian's "confidence to enter" is "by the blood of Jesus" (10:19).

Christ has cut out all middlemen. As a result, even the most feeble saint can enjoy intimate and immediate communion with God through faith in who Jesus was and what Jesus did. Therefore, "let us hold fast the confession of our hope without wavering, for He who promised is faithful" (10:23). (Note the second great cardinal virtue.)

A Christian is not a glorified gambler who leans on the law of averages hoping for a better roll of the dice the next time around. Such comfort isn't Christian, it's pagan. More than that, it's cruel. It asks us to trust in chance. And, frankly, I don't have enough faith to believe in chance. Fortunately, ours is a solid hope full of power and promise, because it rests on the God who promises, believing with boldness, "He who promised is faithful."

Then, there is love. "And let us consider how to stimulate one another to love and good deeds, not forsaking our own assembling together, as is the habit of some, but encouraging one another; and all the more, as you see the day drawing near" (10:24,25). Our ministry of love as Jesus Folk is to care, share and prepare. We are to care in the sense of being involved with our fellow Christians. Watching over one another. Studying how we may stir up, stimulate and incite each other to love, helpful deeds and creative action.

We are to share by being aware of our interdependence. A Christian cannot be what Moffatt called "a pious particle." A Christian in isolation—or selfish Christianity—is a contradiction of terms. To try to preserve love without sharing is to attempt the impossible.

"Faith and hope can be practiced by a solitary soul in a hermit's cell or on a deserted island, but the exercise of love is possible only in community. It must have an object. Thus, the writer of Hebrews urges us to maintain our common Christian worship" (Theodore H. Robinson).[1]

This is very relevant today. It isn't uncommon to hear people say, "I love Christ, but church is a bummer. It turns me off." The book of Hebrews repeats to these twentieth-century pilgrims the same admonition given to those first-century folk who failed to see the importance of a loosely organized body of believers. The local church is not *the* Church for which Christ died, but it is a visible expression of that Church to the world in which we live.

Nowhere does scripture suggest God has abandoned the local church or declared it obsolete. Instead, we are clearly instructed not to neglect meeting together (10:25a). Because we care and share, we are to lovingly prepare each other for the coming of Christ with words of encouragement, enthusiasm and optimistic support. And, we are to do so "all the more, as [we] see the day [of his return] drawing near" (10:25b).

After this warm, rather reassuring word, our author makes a sudden shift from compliment to correction. He sticks in the middle portion of the sandwich. He confronts us with one of the most sober warnings in all of scripture. "For if we go on sinning willfully after receiving the knowledge of the truth, there no longer remains a sacrifice for sins" (10:26).

Few truths are more self-evident than that there are many Christians who don't live like it. Nor, is any Bible teaching clearer than the repeated pronouncement that, sooner or later, spiritual dereliction will be dealt with. Some who have a stunted understanding of God's love would have us believe He winks benignly at the

Christian's waywardness, permitting it to go by unnoticed. Others, with an exaggerated emphasis on the Christian's role in redemption, would have us believe saints who sin following their salvation are irretrievably lost and bound for hell.

Neither of these two extremes is true to scripture. Both are blatant heresies. Nowhere does the Bible even remotely suggest Christians can sin and get away with it. Nor does it teach that born-again children of God who do sin are, or can be, lost.

Like everyone else, a Christian is responsible for his own acts and attitudes. If these lead him into sin, he has two alternatives: Judge himself, repent, meet Christ at the cross, by faith appropriate the forgiveness God offers, and get on with the business of growing into spiritual maturity. Or he can remain in his sin, put off confession to God, wait to be judged by Christ at the judgment seat and, in the process, suffer the dual loss of confidence in the Christian life on earth and reward from the Christian life in heaven.

Depending on which of these alternatives we saved sinners take, we anticipate the second coming of Christ (and co-incidentally, death) as either an occasion of joy or judgment.

In terms of sin and the principle of cause-and-effect, four things are true: Everyone has a choice before the fact; everyone has a choice after the fact; consequences spring from those choices; looking backward and forward is a wise way to keep moving upward.

EVERYONE HAS A CHOICE BEFORE THE FACT

It's amazing how complicated some folk can make the plain, simple teachings of scripture. Hebrews 10:26 is a classic example. ''For if we go on sinning willfully after receiving the knowledge of the truth, there no longer remains a sacrifice for sins.'' What agony of soul and painful divisiveness have been spawned by those who fail to grasp the simple fact that *all* sin is deliberate, and God in His grace has provided for our willfulness.

When it comes to yielding to temptation, everyone has a choice before the fact. To sin or not to sin is the universal option constantly open to us as Christians. It's true, as the Bible explains in Leviticus 4 and 5, that there may be an element of ignorance in our sinning; yet, when we think about it deeply, we must come to the inevitable conclusion that *all* sin is willful. At some point in the process, we become aware of what we're doing and choose to do it anyway.

We may be ignorant of the final outcome—the consequences. We may be ignorant of how diabolically clever the devil is. We may be ignorant of the fact hell is not nearly so nice as the road that leads to it. We may be ignorant of the devastating impact of guilt and a sense of guilt upon the psyche. We may be deluded into thinking some sins are not so sinful, and thus, be defrauded by Satan whose true power we do not fully realize.

But, in spite of these areas of ignorance, somewhere along the line in *every* act of sinning there is a moment of awareness in which we are awakened to the fact we are skating on thin ice. However, despite the Spirit's warning, we deliberately choose to inch a bit closer to the edge.

It's just not possible to divide sin into two classifications: forgivable because done in ignorance, or unforgivable because deliberate. There is a willful element in *all* sin which can neither be denied nor disguised. The more honest, open, sensitive and Spirit-filled a Christian is, the more quickly he will recognize the deliberate nature of his wicked acts. That's why Hebrews 10:26 plagues so many. They take it seriously. And they should!

But, rightly divided, this word of truth will free us rather than frighten us. That right dividing begins by recognizing the verse is speaking of *all* sin. For *all* sin is in some sense deliberate.

There are many ways to sin willfully or "[fall] away from the living God" (3:12). Most commentators want to limit this sin of willfulness to apostasy—the deliberate denial of something once believed. But apostasy itself cannot be limited to the result of intellectual speculation when, in a state of agnostic skepticism, one throws it all over because the Good News boggles his mind.

What about the "falling away" which will not take a burden to the Lord and leave it there? Does that not also involve abandonment of belief in God's promises and His power to keep those promises? What about the deliberate decision not to tithe in the face of God's clear instruction that the first tenth is holy unto Him? What about the refusal to take time to pray or discipline one's mind in a searching study of the scriptures? What about the willful reordering of life's priorities leaving God the last and least instead of the first and best?

All of these attitudes are apostate to one degree or another. They involve lack of trust in God and create a cleavage between Father and child. As someone has declared, sin comes down to a refusal to meet God where He wants to be met, on the terms He Himself has set.

When we sin willfully, as Christians, are we lost? Yes—for the moment—painfully so! But only from our perspective, not from God's. The heavenly Father knows nothing can separate us from Him. He knows nothing can pluck us out of His hand. But in our fallen-away-ness we forget that fact.

Part of the pain sin inflicts on sinner-saints is that, in our shame and regret, we "cast away our confidence." For that moment we forget who we are and Whose we are. We forget why we're here and where we're going. In a most poignant, piercing, personal way, we are lost. We dwell in severe darkness of soul. Hope is all around, but we cannot see it. The shades of our mind, emotion and will are pulled. We do not permit the Light of the World to come in, in a commanding, dominating, darkness-dispelling way.

EVERYONE HAS A CHOICE AFTER THE FACT

When it comes to sin and the principle of cause-and-effect, everyone has a choice *before* the fact. Everyone also has a choice *after* the fact. "For if we go on sinning willfully [which at the deepest level involves *all* sin] after receiving the knowledge of the truth, there no longer remains a sacrifice for sins" (10:26).

Did you notice that between the admonitions at the beginning of chapter 6 (1-12) and the end of chapter 10 (19-39), there is the tremendous development (6:13—10:18) of Christ as high priest functioning in the true tabernacle of God? With our Lord's never-ending ministry of reconciliation in mind, the writer of Hebrews now declares, "If we go on sinning . . . there no longer remains a sacrifice for sins" (10:26).

In essence, he is saying: In Christ, God has done all for us He can do. There is no other Saviour to come and die for sinners. There is no other Jesus to seek and save the lost. So, when, as saved sinners, we are guilty of anything which defiles the image of God in us, or denies the Lordship of Christ over us, there is only one thing we can do—rush to the cross for the forgiveness God offers there *and only there!* There is no other sacrifice for sins.

To sin or not to sin is the universal option constantly open to Christians. To be forgiven or not forgiven when we sin is the urgent question each of us must answer for ourselves. In other words, like everyone else, we Jesus Folk must assume responsibility for our sin and for doing something about it. The only thing we *can* do which has meaning is swallow our pride, do what does not come naturally from the psychological point of view (ego would still like to believe it can go it alone) and turn to the only Saviour for sinners—be they Christian or non-Christian sinners.

The cross is ever and always sufficient for any who rest in it. Its only limitation is the one we set through lack of appropriation and application. *God can do nothing more than forgive us. If we refuse to be forgiven, we must face a fiery purging at the judgment seat of Christ.* The teaching of scripture is just that plain. "For if we go on sinning willfully after receiving the knowledge of the truth, there no longer remains a sacrifice for sins, but a certain terrifying expectation of judgment, and the fury of a fire which will consume the adversaries" (10:26,27).

People read these words and ask, "What do they mean?" I don't wish to sound flippant, but they mean exactly what they say. There is no mystery to the fact that, in a sense, at some point, *all* sin is deliberate. Thus, for Christians who sin following conversion, there is no other place to go for forgiveness and cleansing but Calvary. If we refuse to do business with the gentle Jesus on His cross, we shall do business with Jesus, the Judge, on His throne.

These verses are not a call to faultless living. Only a mediocre person is always at his best. God is well aware of human frailty. And, the Good News is that He has done something about it. Hebrews 10:26,27 is a pronouncement of what He has done, a call to realize all sin defiles the image of God in us and must be dealt with swiftly, lest it harden into a lifestyle, effecting consequences of the severest sort.

CONSEQUENCES SPRING FROM OUR CHOICES

Two things beg to be said about the inevitable and inescapable consequences which spring from the choices we make. First, for Christians who refuse to repent and accept Christ's sacrifice as adequate for their brand of sinning, there is something worse than stoning. "For if we go on sinning willfully after receiving the knowledge of the truth, there no longer remains a sacrifice for sins, but a certain terrifying expectation of judgment, and the fury of a fire which will consume the adversaries. Anyone who has set aside the Law of Moses dies without mercy on the testimony of two or three witnesses.

"How much severer punishment do you think he will deserve who has trampled under foot the Son of God, and has regarded as unclean the blood of the covenant by which he was sanctified, and has insulted the Spirit of grace? For we know Him who said, 'Vengeance is Mine, I will repay.' And again, 'The Lord will judge His people.' It is a terrifying thing to fall into the hands of the living God" (10:26-31).

If there is a passage of scripture anywhere which confronts us with the serious nature of Christian discipleship, it is this one. It's important for us to fully understand it. Among other things, we must see this as an announcement that some Christians will *never* repent of their rebellion as sons of God. As a result, they will be judged accordingly. That judgment is called a "fury of . . . fire" (10:27a), in harmony with Paul's statement to the Corinthians regarding the test of fire to which the Christians' works will be put (I Corinthians 3:13-15).

But notice, the purpose of this "fury of . . . fire" is not to destroy the sinner-saint, but "to consume the adversaries" (10:27b). It is the devil and his devilish work which the judgment fire will devour. Instead of turning His wayward children over to Satan, God in His grace purges them. He produces purified persons suitable for heaven. At the same time, He robs Satan, their adversary, of his intended victims.[3]

Unfortunately, the Christian whose works are burned winds up tragically and sadly empty-handed. The recurring theme of judgment for Jesus Folk threading through Hebrews relates to the Christian's reward, as distinguished from his salvation. Our salvation is by grace—period. Our reward is the accrued and compound interest earned by faithfulness in service and self-giving. The judgment described as a "fury of . . . fire" is not aimed at destroying the impenitent sinner-saint, but at purifying him while, at the same time, denying the devil another victim.

According to custom, violators of the law of Moses were condemned to death by stoning. However, there is something worse than stoning for saved sinners who spurn the Lordship of Jesus. What is it? Having to live with the knowledge of their sin and the fact that there is no possibility of keeping it from Christ, sparing Him the pain sin always inflicts upon Him and His body, the Church.

It is possible for someone, in a moment of weakness or loneliness, to break the marriage vow. If he or she handles that grievous sin redemptively at the cross, there is cleansing for the offend*er*. And, if he or she handles it courageously, bearing the mark and memory of that sin *alone* out of love for his mate, the offend*ed* is protected from the pain knowledge of the broken vow would produce.

But, in the case of our marriage relationship with Christ, there is no way we, His bride, can keep the fact of our willful waywardness and spiritual infidelity from Him. Therefore, when we *remain* unfaithful to Him, we bear a double pain. That which a sense of guilt produces in us and that which the fact of guilt inflicts upon Him.

One who has even a scintilla of spiritual sensitivity finds this a fate worse than stoning.

A further consequence springing from our persistent refusal as Christians to repent and accept the sacrifice of Jesus as adequate for our brand of sin is that God finally takes us at our word. Like the Israelites of old, He permits us to wander off into the wilderness and become "castaway[s]" (I Corinthians 9:27, KJV). The person involved is not eternally lost. It is true, of course, he has lost the confidence and joy of vital Christian living. And, that's painful enough! But worse, his usefulness to God on earth is lost or, at best, limited.

This was the Apostle Paul's great dread (I Corinthians 9:27). What he feared more than anything else was not the loss of his salvation; he knew that was impossible. He was afraid of losing his confidence. His usefulness. His reward. Having proclaimed the Good News to others, he was fearful that, by some act of foolishness or faithlessness, he himself would become disqualified. One whom God had to retire from service until that day when he would be dealt with at the judgment seat of Christ.

Paul knew he would be saved until the end. Would be recognized as one of God's redeemed. Would be made fit for heaven by the refiner's fire. He also knew the wood, hay and stubble of any wasted years would go up in smoke, leaving him to face Jesus with empty hands. The very thought of it made his sensitive soul shudder. It should have the same effect on us!

When we sin and refuse to deal with it creatively at the cross, there is a fate worse than stoning, and we must live with the knowledge of what sin does to us and our Saviour. We must also face the peril of pushing God so far that He will finally disqualify us for further work here on earth.

A fact does not change because it is ignored. One inescapable fact is that Jesus is Someone whom all of us must meet, sooner or later (4:13). He would rather meet us as Saviour and Friend. If we refuse Him on those terms, we shall meet Him as Judge. I'm not trying to scare you. It is impossible to frighten anyone into the kind of loving relationship with Christ characteristic of authentic Christianity. I am simply saying a personal encounter with Christ is inevitable. Sometime, somewhere, you shall meet Him.

A Cockney soldier put it this way. His theology may be a bit off, but his concern is correct:

> There ain't no throne, and there ain't no books,
> It's 'im you gotta see,
> It's 'im, just 'im, that is the judge
> Of blokes like you and me.
>
> And, boys, I'd rather be frizzled up
> In the flames of a burning 'ell,
> Than stand and look into 'is face,
> And 'ear 'is voice say, "Well?"

What a dreadful moment that shall be! How miserably ashamed we shall feel if we miss the path that would have led to peace, joy and wholeness.[2]

The second thing begging to be said about the consequences of our choices is that no child of God need meet Jesus on the terms just described. For the saved sinner who repents of his waywardness and receives God's forgiveness, there is something better than just getting by. There is hope born of the knowledge that God's justice is just.

"For we know Him who said, 'Vengeance is Mine, I will repay.' And again, 'The Lord will judge His people.' It is a terrifying thing to fall into the hands of the living

God" (10:30-31). This text has often been used in an effort to flog the unsaved into action. But remember, these words are found in a passage which refers directly and specifically to Christians! It is "His people" whom the Lord will judge (10:30). But the big news is that this is a word designed to draw you *to* God in confidence, not drive you *from* God in dread. For Christians who trust and obey Him, falling into the hands of the living God will be a glorious experience.

After King David had sinned in his numbering of the people, he was asked to choose between three forms of judgment. His wise reply, based upon previous experience with the grace of God, led him to say, "Let us now fall into the hand of the Lord for His mercies are great" (II Samuel 24:14). When that question is put to us, into whose hands would we rather fall? Those of our fellow humans? Or those of our God from whom no one can pluck us away?

Before whom would we rather stand in judgment? Our fellow man? Or the One who says, "Vengeance is Mine, I will repay"? While it's true no flimsy excuse or pleading of the fifth amendment will get us by on that occasion, one thing is sure: God's justice is just!

This is our hope. Jesus will see us through. He not only knows what we do, but why. He knows those things which inhibit faith. He knows the glandular excesses which make some so nervous they just cannot rest in Him. He knows the physical deficiencies which make some so morose they cannot enjoy their walk in the Spirit. He knows the ebb and flow of bodily functions so characteristic of this complicated piece of fleshy plumbing in which our spirit dwells, a tidal cycle so violent at times we are wholly preoccupied with ourselves. He knows all of that.

I remember talking with a leading psychiatrist in

Chicago. He had a beautiful office on the twentieth floor of a building overlooking a park and Lake Michigan. It offered a spectacular view of water, flowers and trees. As we chatted about the kind of helping ministry that might occur through a wedding of his discipline and mine, he commented on this turned-in-ness of people. "You know, John, there are some folk who, when they come in to see me, are so distressed, so preoccupied with themselves and their feelings, they can look out this window at this magnificent view and never even see it."

How many times have you been so caught up in distress of soul you weren't aware the sun was shining? Or the flowers growing? Or the birds singing? Well, our Lord, who knows the end from the beginning and everything in between, is aware of the factors affecting faith. He knows those childhood influences which so brutalize some people they are plagued by feelings of inadequacy, fear of failure and dread of life in general until it's virtually impossible for them to experience even a modicum of the joy and peace Jesus came to give.

I'm grateful the One who will judge me is Jesus. I'm glad it is God's hand into which I shall fall. For if there's anything I know to be absolutely certain, it's this: God's great longing is to be our Friend as well as our Father. If we come to Him by faith, claiming the cleansing He offers, falling into His hands—the hands of our living and loving Lord—will be a glorious and healing experience.

LOOKING BACKWARD AND FORWARD IS A WISE WAY TO KEEP MOVING FORWARD

"But remember the former days, when, after being enlightened, you endured a great conflict of sufferings, partly by being made a public spectacle through reproaches and tribulations, and partly by becoming sharers with those who were so treated. For you showed sympathy to the prisoners, and accepted joyfully the seizure of your property, knowing that you have for yourselves a better possession and an abiding one.

"Therefore, do not throw away your confidence, which has a great reward. For you have need of endurance, so that when you have done the will of God, you may receive what was promised. For yet in a very little while, He who is coming will come and will not delay. But My righteous one shall live by faith; And if he shrinks back, My soul has no pleasure in him. But we are not of those who shrink back to destruction, but of those who have faith to the preserving of the soul" (10:32-39).

With what comfort and encouragement this admonition closes! Our author completes the sandwich: compliment, correction, compliment. As in chapter 6 (9-12), he ends chapter 10 on a hopeful note. He is a Good News man.

He says to his struggling, fellow sinner-saints, "Remember the days of old. Remember your first love. Remember the absolute confidence you had that anything was possible through Christ. Rekindle your first love if it has grown cold. Remember the joy of your earlier years of sacrifice and service. Recall how you came through the severest tests with flying colors.

"Don't sell yourself short. Don't believe the devil's lie that the worst things about you are the only true things about you. In the past, you met grievous challenge to your faith, stood firm and won. Your hope of heaven helped you then. Let it help you now. Throw off your current spiritual indolence. Get caught up in the growing process again. Be an imitator of those who through faith gained the golden crown. And you, too, will reap a harvest of inexpressible joy."

The writer of Hebrews doesn't stop with this appeal to

a backward look. He urges them to take a forward look also. They are to be retrospective. To remember how far they've come in Christ and to gain encouragement from that. But they are also to be pro-spective. They must remember where they are headed and be inspired by that.

"Jesus is coming soon," he says. "You'll not have long to wait. In view of that fact, hang tough! Evaluate everything in the light of His coming. Keep your record behind you, your hope before you, and you will emerge from the tests through which you are now passing stronger and better than ever."

Need I point out the message in that for us today? Jesus is coming soon. I know some doubters argue that Christians have been claiming this for 2,000 years, and that two millenia ago Christ said He would come back soon and He isn't here yet. They infer this promise cannot be trusted. As God measures time, in which a thousand years are as a day, it's been less than two days since Jesus said He would return shortly! He hasn't broken His promise. Yet a little while and He will come. Keep that fact in mind. Learn to live with eternity's values in view and you'll be liberated from the tyranny of the present.

While you're looking forward, look backward. Remember where you were when you began the Christian life and how far you've come by the grace of God. Gain encouragement from that. Don't throw away your confidence. Throw off your spiritual sluggishness. Keep the faith, and with it, confidence in Christ. Claim His sacrifices as wholly adequate for your sin. In this way, you'll be able to anticipate His coming as an occasion of joy, not judgment.

When George Mallory, the famed mountain climber, failed to return from his fatal attempt at conquering Mount Everest, a group of newsmen asked the other climbers what had happened to him. I was greatly impressed with their reply. They said: "When last seen, he was still going strong toward the top." God grant that we may possess the grace of continuance so that when our days on earth are done, it also may be said of each of us: "He perished in the pursuit of his goal. He was pressing onward. His face was upward. His heart was set on conquering. And when last seen, he was still going strong toward the top."

8

HOW TO
Hang Tough in
a Hostile World

Hebrews 11:1–12:3

NOW faith is the assurance of things hoped for, the conviction of things not seen. ²For by it the men of old gained approval. ³By faith we understand that the worlds were prepared by the word of God, so that what is seen was not made out of things which are visible. ⁴By faith Abel offered to God a better sacrifice than Cain, through which he obtained the testimony that he was righteous, God testifying about his gifts, and through faith, though he is dead, he still speaks.

⁵By faith Enoch was taken up so that he should not see death; and he was not found because God took him up; for he obtained the witness that before his being taken up he was pleasing to God. ⁶And without faith it is impossible to please Him, for he who comes to God must believe that He is, and that He is a rewarder of those who seek Him.

⁷By faith Noah, being warned by God about things not yet seen, in reverence prepared an ark for the salvation of his household, by which he condemned the world, and became an heir of the righteousness which is according to faith.

⁸*By faith Abraham, when he was called, obeyed by going out to a place which he was to receive for an inheritance; and he went out, not knowing where he was going.* ⁹*By faith he lived as an alien in the land of promise, as in a foreign land, dwelling in tents with Isaac and Jacob, fellow-heirs of the same promise;* ¹⁰*for he was looking for the city which has foundations, whose architect and builder is God.* ¹¹*By faith even Sarah herself received ability to conceive, even beyond the proper time of life, since she considered Him faithful who had promised;* ¹²*therefore, also, there was born of one man, and him as good as dead at that, as many descendants as the stars of heaven in number, and innumerable as the sand which is by the seashore.*

¹³*All these died in faith, without receiving the promises, but having seen them and having welcomed them from a distance, and having confessed that they were strangers and exiles on the earth.* ¹⁴*For those who say such things make it clear that they are seeking a country of their own.* ¹⁵*And indeed if they had been thinking of that country from which they went out, they would have had opportunity to return.* ¹⁶*But as it is, they desire a better country, that is a heavenly one. Therefore God is not ashamed to be called their God; for He has prepared a city for them.*

¹⁷*By faith Abraham, when he was tested, offered up Isaac; and he who had received the promises was offering up his only begotten son;* ¹⁸*it was he to whom it was said, "In Isaac your seed shall be called."* ¹⁹*He considered that God is able to raise men even from the dead; from which he also received him back as a type.*

²⁰*By faith Isaac blessed Jacob and Esau, even regarding things to come.* ²¹*By faith Jacob, as he was dying, blessed each of the sons of Joseph, and*

worshiped, leaning on the top of his staff. ²²By faith Joseph, when he was dying, made mention of the exodus of the sons of Israel, and gave orders concerning his bones.

²³By faith Moses, when he was born, was hidden for three months by his parents, because they saw he was a beautiful child; and they were not afraid of the king's edict. ²⁴By faith Moses, when he had grown up, refused to be called the son of Pharaoh's daughter; ²⁵choosing rather to endure ill-treatment with the people of God, than to enjoy the passing pleasures of sin; ²⁶considering the reproach of Christ greater riches than the treasures of Egypt; for he was looking to the reward. ²⁷By faith he left Egypt, not fearing the wrath of the king; for he endured, as seeing Him who is unseen. ²⁸By faith he kept the Passover and the sprinkling of the blood, so that he who destroyed the first-born might not touch them. ²⁹By faith they passed through the Red Sea as though they were passing through dry land; and the Egyptians, when they attempted it, were drowned.

³⁰By faith the walls of Jericho fell down, after they had been encircled for seven days. ³¹By faith Rahab the harlot did not perish along with those who were disobedient, after she had welcomed the spies in peace.

³²And what more shall I say? For time will fail me if I tell of Gideon, Barak, Samson, Jephthah, of David and Samuel and the prophets, ³³who by faith conquered kingdoms, performed acts of righteousness, obtained promises, shut the mouths of lions, ³⁴quenched the power of fire, escaped the edge of the sword, from weakness were made strong, became mighty in war, put foreign armies to flight.

³⁵Women received back their dead by resurrection; and others were tortured, not accepting their

138

release, in order that they might obtain a better resurrection; [36]*and others experienced mockings and scourgings, yes, also chains and imprisonment.* [37]*They were stoned, they were sawn in two, they were tempted, they were put to death with the sword; they went about in sheepskins, in goatskins, being destitute, afflicted, ill-treated* [38]*(men of whom the world was not worthy), wandering in deserts and mountains and caves and holes in the ground.* [39]*And all these, having gained approval through their faith, did not receive what was promised,* [40]*because God had provided something better for us, so that apart from us they should not be made perfect.*

[1]*Therefore, since we have so great a cloud of witnesses surrounding us, let us also lay aside every encumbrance, and the sin which so easily entangles us, and let us run with endurance the race that is set before us.*

[2]*Fixing our eyes on Jesus the author and perfecter of faith, who for the joy set before Him endured the cross, despising the shame, and has sat down at the right hand of the throne of God.*

[3]*For consider Him who has endured such hostility by sinners against Himself, so that you may not grow weary and lose heart.*

The week prior to my writing the sermon which served as basic research for this chapter had been most exhilarating and demanding, reminding me again of my inability to be all things to all men. I had tried hard to be father to my children, especially my daughter who was home from college for a few hours. Husband to my wife. Pastor to my flock. A worthy minister of God to the community. A faithful student of God's written and living Word. Yet, it was a week in which I had been unable to "get it all together."

Preaching has always been excruciatingly difficult for me. Some men seem to have a natural pulpit gift. My effectiveness, if there be any, has come as the product of hard work. And, while I labor diligently over every sermon, rarely have I struggled with a message as much as the one in question.

When I finished writing my message on Friday, I threw up my hands in horror and informed my secretary I would have to re-do the whole thing. It just wouldn't jell. I struggled with it Friday evening and all day Saturday. Finally, about 11:00 p.m. I was so exhausted I said, "Well, God, I don't know what's behind all this, but I'll just have to leave this unfinished sermon with You and get some sleep. I'm weary to the bone."

About 11:30, I drifted off to sleep. After sleeping about five, possibly ten, minutes the phone rang. It was a person gravely concerned about a friend in the Los

Angeles area who had called long distance to say she was contemplating suicide. This person didn't quite know what to say or do to help her friend. We spent some time on the phone devising a plan whereby some support could be given by long distance, and contacts were made for additional support where the troubled friend lived.

I tried to go back to sleep and had just drifted off when the telephone rang a second time. It was another lady, one whom I did not know, who also had come to such a crisis point in her life she questioned whether life was worth continuing. For the better part of an hour, I ministered to her over the telephone. We prayed together.

I hung up the phone and, though I needed sleep badly, I was bug-eyed. So I lay there praying for the people who had been brought to my attention. After a time, my prayer turned to asking God for some insight as to what this was all about.

He said, "Son, what is the primary crisis these people are facing?"

"Well, Father," I replied, "it looks to me like a crisis of faith."

He answered, "That's right. And many of My children are going through similar crises. I've let you struggle with the demands of this week, an unfinished sermon and these midnight calls as My way of telling you that, at long last, the time has come for you to share with others your own personal struggle in learning how to walk by faith."

And that's what I did. If I looked tired that Sunday morning—I was. But the fatigue was only physical. Spiritually, I was riding on the front bumper. To have more joy, I would have had to be two people. When the services were over, we all knew God had done something great in our midst. My sharing had been used to fortify others in their faith. The substance of that sharing is included as part of this chapter, with the hope it will make this subject especially helpful.

The completed Jews to whom the book of Hebrews was originally addressed were having a tough time of it. When they turned from Judaism to Jesus, they laid down—ever so tentatively— the comfortable old security blanket of temple life with its bustling priesthood and carefully structured ritual sacrifice. In place of these visible, physical, religious activities on earth, they substituted the invisible, spiritual ministry of Jesus in heaven. As Christians, their life was to center in things hoped for and unseen. But now they were being pressured from every imaginable angle to revert to the familiar patterns and practices of pre-Christian days.

Could they withstand this pressure? Could they survive and grow strong without the religious props they had once depended upon? Could they hang tough in a hostile world? The writer of Hebrews says, "Yes—provided you walk by faith, not sight."

Our situation is not dissimilar to theirs. The scenery has changed. We are not asked to forsake animal sacrifices and ritual cleansings. These have never been part of our religious paraphernalia. But we are asked to ". . . walk by faith, not by sight" (II Corinthians 5:7). To move out into a dangerous, difficult world and maintain the keen edge of our Christian commitment and conviction. We are asked to trust God on what strikes some as slim evidence He even is. To walk by faith when the tendency of our time is to play it safe. To venture all for Christ when every secular voice we hear says self-sacrifice is stupid.

How are we to function in such an atmosphere? How are we to keep our goals in focus, our priorities in proper order? We are to do as the ancients did. We are to follow the instruction given to those first-century fledglings. We are to walk by faith, not by sight.

DESCRIPTION, NOT DEFINITION

What is faith? It is "the assurance of things hoped for, the conviction of things not seen" (11:1).

It is important to note that what our writer gives us here is a description rather than a definition of faith. A definition is formal and exact. It includes all that belongs to the word being defined. It excludes all that doesn't. A description, on the other hand, is not formal or exact. Nor is it all-inclusive. Rather, it is a word picture which spotlights certain special features of that which is being described. Because our author is more concerned with what faith does than with what faith is, he gives us a description instead of a definition.

The writer of Hebrews sees faith as that fruit of the Spirit which will keep Jesus Folk alive and well in a hostile world, without dependency upon visual aids of any kind. Faith will spare us the pain and loss of becoming spiritual dropouts. It will keep us keeping on. Help us run with patience the race set before us. In other words, this entire eleventh chapter of Hebrews must be seen in relationship to the underlying concern which threads throughout the entire book: God's concern that we, His children, persevere in the face of all kinds of pressure.

Elsewhere in scripture we are told how, through other facets of faith, we can stand before God in heaven. Here we are told how, through a mature, triumphant faith, we can stand before men on earth. According to his description, faith enables the Jesus person to know what other people do not know. To believe what mere mortals do not believe. And, to act upon that knowledge and belief.

Faith is not wishful thinking. It is not operating on a hunch. Or hoping for the best. Or acting foolishly when common sense and good judgment dictate otherwise. Faith does not renounce reason. It reaches beyond it to discover those realities which reason alone can never perceive. Faith does not see what isn't there. It sees all that is there. It knows there is more to life than meets the eye. And, it puts us in touch with those things which, though invisible, are truly real.

"Now faith is the assurance of things hoped for" (11:1a). It enables us Jesus people to know with certainty what other folk can only surmise. Best of all, it permits us to experience the reality of those things for which we hope—here and now. The "assurance [or realization] of things hoped for" is nothing more or less than the sure confidence that that which we shall appropriate fully in the future can be experienced and rejoiced in, at least in part, today. Knowing that is knowing what ordinary people do not know. The certainty that the better things for which we long are, in their beginnings, already present only comes through faith.

Faith is further "the conviction of things not seen" (11:1b). It enables God's children to believe what mere mortals do not believe. The secular world says seeing is believing. The spiritual world says believing is seeing. Faith operates on the premise that unseen things are not less real than seen things. Love, for instance, is not less real than lead. Sound is not less real than sod. As a matter of fact, it is the conviction of faith that spiritual things are *more* vital than material things. They are truly real.

Faith provides the Jesus person with convincing proof the unseen world, about which the writer of Hebrews has been talking in chapters 8-10, is the supreme reality. By faith, the soul sees what the eye cannot see. The heart hears what the ear cannot hear. The spirit understands what the mind cannot comprehend. Which is to say, faith empowers the Christian to believe what mere mortals cannot believe: the ultimate reality of things unseen.

But faith is more than knowledge and belief. It involves positive action upon the truth known and the promise believed. Faith is never idle waiting. It is always belief and knowledge acting. Acting on what? The writer of Hebrews replies: the credibility of God. "[For] without faith it is impossible to please Him, for he who comes to God must believe that He is and that He is a rewarder of those who seek Him" (11:6).

The reason triumphant faith sees the invisible, hears the inaudible, believes the incredible and receives the impossible is because it is rooted in the God of Promises and in the promises of God. Faith is not the stuff of which daydreams are made. Faith is not a stained glass word. Faith is a tough-fibered, bare-knuckled thing which is convinced beyond any possible doubt that God is altogether worthy of our trust. Triumphant faith is not belief in the existence of any god, it is belief in the existence of *the* God who makes promises and keeps them!

Now, lack of faith was the problem of those first-century Jesus Folk. It is our problem, too. As a matter of fact, lack of faith has been mankind's problem from the time of Adam and Eve. Sin is not disobedience. It is disbelief. The opposite of sin is not obedience. It is faith. Obedience is the by-product of a faith relationship. Disobedience is the inevitable result of the fracturing of a faith relationship.

The first sin recorded in Genesis was not Eve's act of disobedience in eating the forbidden fruit. The *original* sin was unbelief. Before she ever disobeyed God, Eve disbelieved God. The serpent made more sense to her than the loving Father. She took Satan's word over that of God, and the sin of disbelief led to disobedience.

That's why faith is so important to God. That's why, without faith, it is impossible to please God. Faith is the opposite of sin. Faith is that act whereby we venture our eternal interest on the bare word of God, believing Him solely on the basis of what He has said without asking for proof. And until we have given God that kind of unconditional trust, we haven't really given Him anything.

This is something I learned rather late in life. For most questing Christians, there are three stages of faith. At the beginning there is the uncritical stage, in which the experience of Jesus is so direct and compelling the questions have not yet had a chance to surface. Then there is the middle, or critical, stage of faith, when the questions come faster than the answers. We find the so-called simple gospel is not so simple after all.

Finally, there is the post-critical stage when, having been subjected to the fire of testing, faith emerges from the crucible more sturdy than ever before. Like a bone which has been broken, tested faith is stronger once it is healed. Stronger because it refused to run from the questions. Stronger because it was willing to face the darts of doubt. But, while becoming stronger, the period of brokenness and healing can be extremely painful.

It was during a spasm of that middle stage of faith that I came close to quitting the ministry a few years ago. I grew up in a highly rationalistic era when blind faith was widely ridiculed. To believe anything upon pure faith alone was considered unintelligent. Therefore, it was exceedingly important to me that I have a logical, defensible reason—unfettered and unfortified by faith—for the hope which was within me.

I was gripped by a desperate need to know. To have every question answered. Every issue carefully catalogued and pigeonholed with the "proper" response. And, for a number of years I got away with that kind of infantile concept of Christianity. Then, suddenly, for reasons far too complex to detail here, I was catapulted into situations in which I faced questions I could not answer. Issues I could not resolve.

I was in a terrible dilemma. I had not learned to "walk

by faith." And I was no longer able to "walk by sight." My carefully structured, neatly pigeonholed caricature of Christianity had been shot out from under me. I was legless. Immobile. A spiritual paraplegic. Things deteriorated to a point where I actually questioned the existence of God. I didn't deny Him. I simply awoke one day to discover I no longer believed in Him.

Now, ministers are not supposed to doubt. At least, not doubt the existence of God. So I fought off facing the crisis of this middle stage of faith for several months. I went through all the right motions and said all the right words. During this period, people were converted to Christ and the church was blessed. Remember, God's promise is to honor His word (Isaiah 55:11), not the person who proclaims it. Yet, despite the outward blessings, I was dead inside. Finally, it came to a point where I felt morally and ethically I could no longer take God's money to tell people what they wanted to hear when I didn't believe myself. I decided to leave the ministry.

At that point I took Lucille into my confidence for the first time, because a decision of that sort would have a profound effect on her. It would mean loss of income, home, and the minimal amount of security the ministry affords. In fact, it would result in chaos for our entire family.

I remember vividly the Saturday night I asked her to ride with me into the country. I described the deep distress of soul through which I had been going. She listened empathetically. She didn't preach to me. Or inundate me with proof texts. She shared that she, too, had gone through periods of doubt and promised to pray for me.

The following Sunday morning I went through the first service, and, as I recall, people were converted. But inwardly I was miserable. When worship was over, I rushed into my study, locked the door, put my head on my desk and said, "God, if there is a God, you have one hour to make Yourself real to me. Unless something happens in the next sixty minutes, I shall have to announce at the second service my decision to resign the ministry."

It's interesting I should have had that kind of conversation. As I reflect upon it now, it indicates I was not an atheist, or even a deist. I was simply caught in the agony and uncertainty of the middle stage of faith. The crisis point for me up to that time was an inability to walk by faith. I could walk by reason. Or logic. Or sight. But by faith? No! That was impossible.

As I sat there pondering my dilemma, a portion of scripture came to mind. It had been cropping up repeatedly for a number of weeks. "He who comes to God must believe that He is [exists], and that He is a rewarder of those who seek Him" (11:6b).

"But, God, that's my problem," I argued. "I'm not sure You really are."

And God said—now, I didn't hear a voice, but the conversation was as real as any I have ever experienced, "There's more to that verse; please look it up."

I went to a concordance, searched out a key word, found Hebrews 11:6, and turning to my Bible, read: "And without faith it is impossible to please Him, for he who comes to God must believe that He is and that He is a rewarder of those who seek Him." *Without faith it is impossible to please Him!*

My reaction was quick and angry. "Thanks a lot, God! This just makes matters worse. My problem is that I'm short on faith. The very thing You want is what I can't give." Then I asked, "God, why is it so important to You that I give You faith?"

And He answered my question with one of His own. "John, why is it important that your son have faith in you?''

I answered, "That's obvious. If Jeff didn't have faith in me, there would be no possibility of a meaningful relationship between us. Life would be impossible if every time we sat down to dinner he said, 'Has anybody run a chemical analysis on this food? Mom, you say it's fit to eat, but how do I know for sure? Dad, you take the first bite and prove it to me.' Or suppose he questioned everything I said. Doubted every comment I made. Asked for proof before he would accept the truth of the things I try to teach him. Why, it would be impossible to have any meaningful relationship with my son unless he had faith in me.''

Even as I gave God the answer to His question, I had the answer to my own. "Now I see what You're trying to tell me, God. You're saying the reason it isn't possible to please You without faith is because without faith there isn't any substance or meaning to our relationship.'' I began to realize that until I gave God unconditional faith in the absence of answers, I hadn't really given Him anything. I had given Him my life. My talent. My money. My family. But, I had not given Him unconditional trust.

Again, I put my head on my desk, "God, if there is a God, from this point on I surrender the need to know. By a deliberate act of the will, I commit myself to walk by faith, not sight.'' As I continued to pray, I was at first surrounded and then ultimately filled with an overwhelming sense of the reality of God. I was gripped by "the conviction of things not seen,'' and given an assurance that God is, which has not left from that day to this.

For decades I had tried to come to terms with my doubt. That morning I decided to come to terms with my faith. As a result, I passed from the desperate agony of questions I could not answer to the exquisite agony of answers I cannot escape. And it has been wonderful!

I don't mean to imply all my problems were over. To the contrary. Since then I have faced the severest tests of my lifetime. I have made many serious mistakes. On occasion, I have gravely strained my fellowship with God. But, there has never been one moment when I doubted my relationship to God. I am convinced that, in His foreknowledge, my heavenly Father knew of the crises ahead and prepared me for them in advance by permitting me to go through that earlier, agonizing middle stage of faith in which I learned beyond any shadow of doubt that God is, and that He rewards those who earnestly seek Him.

Like a bone which has been broken, tested faith is stronger once it is healed. It surrenders the need to know and in the process knows as never before. It gives up a dependency on proof and winds up with a form of proof which boggles the mind. It ventures everything on the bare word of God and discovers that this, though it defies reason, is altogether reasonable.

Faith, as the writer of Hebrews asserts, boils down to confidence in the credibility of God. Confidence in His living and written word for knowledge about Himself, rather than our own reasoned arguments. Confidence in His grace for the forgiveness of sin, rather than our own feeble efforts to right the wrongs. Confidence in His loving us, rather than our loving Him. In His choosing us, rather than our choosing Him.

Faith rests in God. In His hold on us, rather than our hold on Him. Faith knows and believes, but it also acts on what it knows and believes, and in the process, possesses ". . . the assurance of things hoped for, the conviction of things not seen" (11:1). As someone has said, "In the life of faith, proof and practice go hand in hand. The proof of faith is in the living of faith."

DEMONSTRATION

From this beautiful description, our author moves on to a demonstration of faith. Many commentators have written extensively and well about the people, places and events mentioned in the remaining thirty-nine verses of chapter 11. It will not be necessary for me to do so. Suffice it to say, these verses are laced with rich veins of spiritual ore which will readily yield their treasure to the patient and prayerful student.

I should only like to point out that the folk mentioned here were not selected at random nor picked by accident. The Holy Spirit guided this listing, because all of these people had certain things in common. Not the least of these was the fact that they had gone through the very things those first-century believers were being asked to go through. To leave the familiar and comfortable. To adventure into the unknown. To live with a minimum of security. To court danger and invite hostility. To go forward on the bare word of God. And, by faith, they had done just that.

The facets of faith which carried them through are those described by the writer of Hebrews. They believed in the God of promises—"that He is [exists]" (11:6b). They believed in the promises of God—"that He is a rewarder of those who seek Him" (11:6c). Though the promises God gave them were all in the future, these people acted as if they were already operational; thus, they had the joy of doing and being something great for God. They experienced "the assurance [or realization] of things hoped for" (11:1a). They believed there is more to life than meets the eye. They possessed "the conviction of things not seen" (11:1b). As a result, they were able to hang tough in a hostile world in the face of all kinds of logical and appealing reasons not to do so.

But the most endearing thing they had in common with

those first-century Jesus Folk—was their humanity. Not one of these people was perfect. They all had character flaws. Several were cunning connivers. One was a harlot. All were most unlikely candidates for sainthood. Without exception, they stumbled and fell. But—they did not stay down. Despite their humanity and hang-ups, they refused to roll over and play dead for the devil. When they were down, they got up. When they were going the wrong direction, they did an about face. When they pushed ahead of God and fouled up His program, they got back in His will and out of His way. They could have dropped out, but they didn't. In the face of insurmountable problems and unbelievable obstacles, by faith they pushed on. They hung tough in a hostile world.

If they could do it, so can you, says the author of Hebrews. To be sure, you're being asked to make major sacrifices for your Christian faith. To break with everything comfortable and familiar. To risk alienation from family and friends. To adventure into the unknown with no guarantee of safe return. But, this is nothing new. The history of God's working with His children is crowded with those who walked by faith, not sight. People who had nothing but the promises of God to go on and yet went forth, not knowing where they were going or what they would find when they got there. They came to their extremity and found it to be God's opportunity. They stepped out in blind faith and proved God to be altogether worthy of their trust. If you will take a similar leap of faith, he says, you, too, will hang tough in a hostile world.

DEDUCTION

"Therefore, since we have so great a cloud of witnesses surrounding us, let us also lay aside every encumbrance, and the sin which so easily entangles us, and let us run with endurance the race that is set before us, fixing our eyes on Jesus, the author and perfecter of faith, who for the joy set before Him endured the cross, despising the shame, and has sat down at the right hand of the throne of God. For consider Him who has endured such hostility by sinners against Himself, so that you may not grow weary and lose heart" (12:1-3).

This is the conclusion toward which our author has been pointing from the opening line of his letter. Underlying every carefully honed argument and patiently polished phrase is his practical concern for the spiritual survival of God's earthly offspring. If you miss the "So what?" element which pops up again and again throughout this epistle, you miss the primary thrust of the book. The whole argument is lost unless you realize *we are told who Jesus is and what Jesus did in order that we might avoid the ten deadly dangers of:*

Drift instead of decision (2:1-4)

Hardened hearts instead of help in time of need (3:7—4:16)

Spiritual infantilism instead of Christian growth (5:11—6:3)

Laxity instead of loyalty (6:4-20; 10:26-31; 12:15-17)

Wavering instead of boldness (10:19-23)

Isolationism instead of fellowship (10:24,25)

Weariness instead of endurance (10:26-39)

Comfort instead of discipline (12:1-11)

Dull indifference instead of grateful response (12:25-29)

Expediency instead of eternity (13:1-15)

God is concerned about the spiritual survival and success of His children. He has used the writer of Hebrews in a remarkable way to provide Christian earthlings with the necessary fortification to stand against the storm. To keep on day after day after day. Whether we're successful or not. Whether we're appreciated or not. Whether we're recognized or not. For, as the song says, "This world is not our home, we're just a passin' through."

Others have run the same race. Abraham. Moses. Samuel. David. The prophets. The list goes on and on. They all persisted in faith and are now in the great grandstand of heaven rooting us on. They are not passive onlookers. They are intimately and personally involved in the outcome. Until all have finished the race, none shall receive the prize (11:39,40).

But along with this quite proper personal concern, there is an overriding interest in the ultimate outcome of the whole event. Relay runners, having passed the baton to those who run succeeding laps, do not lose interest in what happens after they have had their run. Instead, they are concerned that all run well for the sake of the corporate effort. The great cloud of witnesses in glory share the same concern. They join Jesus in keen concern that we, too, "run with endurance the race that is set before us" (12:1b).

Furthermore, this "cloud of witnesses" are not mere spectators. Their supreme purpose as rooters is to witness to us as runners. Rather than their looking at us, *we* are to look at *them*. We are to remember the many dangers, toils and snares through which they, by faith, have already come. We are to remember how they learned to "lay aside every weight" which might hinder faith.

Most important of all, we are never, never, never to forget how, through faith, they conquered the sin which clings so closely—the ever present temptation to quit before the race is done. *That's* "the sin which doth so easily beset us" (12:1, KJV). It's the sin of slipping back. Of dropping out. Of failing to "hang tough in a hostile world."

This sin is mentioned repeatedly in Hebrews. Again and again, we are warned against it. The Christian life is not a sprint. It is an endurance run. It requires sustained commitment, lest in falling by the wayside, we lose the satisfaction of doing well while the race is on and also miss the prize to be awarded when the race is done.

Therefore, those who were witnessed of in Hebrews 11 are now witnesses in Hebrews 12 to those of us still on the course. We are challenged to survey the achievements of these past heroes of faith, and to learn by their example. To face our contest with similar concentration and endurance. And, if this "great . . . cloud of witnesses" does not provide sufficient fortification against fatigue, despondency and collapse, we also have the privilege of "fixing our eyes on Jesus . . ." (12:2).

Don't you love the way the writer of Hebrews never misses an opportunity to slip in his favorite theme! Even when making a practical application, he can't resist the temptation to put in a good word for Jesus. "The author and perfecter of faith" (12:2b). The One who has the first word and the last. "The Alpha and the Omega" (Revelation 1:8), Who will never be superseded as either Saviour or Keeper.

The author of Hebrews says, "If all other motivation fails, and you are still strongly tempted to give up the race, look to Jesus who, for the joy that was set before Him, endured far greater strain than you shall ever know. He now roots for you so that you, too, may share His joy and crown."

Is your reaction: "Big deal! Why shouldn't He be able to stick it out? Jesus was God"? True. God *was* in Christ (II Corinthians 5:19). But no mention is made here of that part of His person. It is Jesus to Whom we are to look, not Christ. That's an important distinction. Christ is the name used to describe His deity. Jesus is the name

155

used to depict His humanity. And it is Jesus to Whom we are to look. Jesus—the true Man—who by faith, which is the opposite of sin, obeyed, endured, and gained the victory.

Oh, with what incredible care the Holy Spirit has guided the mind of His earthly scribe! He has taken pains to guard so small a detail as the very name of the One to Whom we are to look for power to persevere. We are to look to Jesus, who as true Man is a picture in living color of what we through faith can be.

In a roundabout way, this brings us back to the basic meaning of faith. It is confidence in another. It is knowing God exists. It is believing He is absolutely worthy of our trust. It is acting upon that knowledge and belief to keep on keeping on, come what may. This is the way to enjoy the present reality of "things hoped for" and possess the sure conviction that the truly real and dependable is often "not seen."

During the London blitz, a father took his little girl to a bomb shelter. The ladder was broken, so he jumped down and stood in the darkness below. It was pitch black. The child, who was still at the top, couldn't see him, though he could make her out dimly against the night sky.

"Jump, dear, jump," he called.

She responded with great anxiety, "But, Daddy, I can't see you. I can't see you."

"Yes, darling, I know. But I can see *you*. Now, jump!"

So, in faith, she leaped into the darkness, to discover she had leaped into the strong security of her father's arms.

Are you inundated by doubt? Are you tempted to quit the race? You can hang tough in this hostile world if you'll just take the leap of faith. I promise you—from personal experience—you won't be disappointed.

9

God Dares to Discipline

Hebrews 12:3-29

FOR consider Him who has endured such hostility by sinners against Himself, so that you may not grow weary and lose heart. ⁴You have not yet resisted to the point of shedding blood in your striving against sin; ⁵and you have forgotten the exhortation which is addressed to you as sons,

"My son, do not regard lightly the discipline of the Lord,

Nor faint when you are reproved by Him;

⁶For those whom the Lord loves He disciplines,

And He scourges every son whom He receives."

⁷It is for discipline that you endure; God deals with you as with sons; for what son is there whom his father does not discipline? ⁸But if you are without discipline, of which all have become partakers, then you are illegitimate children and not sons. ⁹Furthermore, we had earthly fathers to discipline us, and we repected them; shall we not much rather be subject to the Father of spirits, and live? ¹⁰For they disciplined us for a short time as seemed best to them, but He disciplines us for our good, that we may share His holiness.

¹¹All discipline for the moment seems not to be joyful, but sorrowful; yet to those who have been trained by it, afterwards it yields the peaceful fruit

of righteousness. [12]*Therefore, strengthen the hands that are weak and the knees that are feeble, [13]and make straight paths for your feet, so that the limb which is lame may not be put out of joint, but rather be healed.* [14]*Pursue after peace with all men, and after the sanctification without which no one will see the Lord.*

[15]*See to it that no one comes short of the grace of God; that no root of bitterness springing up causes trouble, and by it many be defiled;* [16]*that there be no immoral or godless person like Esau, who sold his own birthright for a single meal.* [17]*For you know that even afterwards, when he desired to inherit the blessing, he was rejected, for he found no place for repentance, though he sought for it with tears.*

[18]*For you have not come to a mountain that may be touched and to a blazing fire, and to darkness and gloom and whirlwind,* [19]*and to the blast of a trumpet and the sound of words which sound was such that those who heard begged that no further word should be spoken to them.* [20]*For they could not bear the command, "If even a beast touches the mountain, it will be stoned."* [21]*And so terrible was the sight, that Moses said, "I am full of fear and trembling."* [22]*But you have come to Mount Zion and to the city of the living God, the heavenly Jerusalem, and to myriads of angels,* [23]*to the general assembly and church of the first-born who are enrolled in heaven, and to God, the judge of all, and to the spirits of righteous men made perfect,* [24]*and to Jesus, the mediator of a new covenant, and to the sprinkled blood, which speaks better than the blood of Abel.*

[25]*See to it that you do not refuse him who is speaking. For if those did not escape when they refused him who warned them on earth, much less shall we escape who turn away from Him who*

warns from heaven. [26]And His voice shook the earth then, but now He has promised, saying, "Yet once more I will shake not only the earth, but also the heaven." [27]And this expression, "Yet once more," denotes the removing of those things which can be shaken, as of created things, in order that those things which cannot be shaken may remain.

[28]Therefore, since we receive a kingdom which cannot be shaken, let us show gratitude, by which we may offer to God an acceptable service with reverence and awe; [29]for our God is a consuming fire.

It was Christmas. The toy department in the big city store was clogged with parents and kids. One little boy was creating a problem for everyone, particularly his mother. He would climb on a trike or wagon and charge down the aisle, bumping into other people. His mother, who had completely lost control of him, trotted alongside saying, "Now, darling, don't do that. Come along now. It's time for us to leave." The youngster paid no heed.

The department head became sufficiently frustrated, went over and said, "Madam, it appears you're having a bit of trouble with your boy. We have a child psychologist on our staff. Would you mind if I invited him to come over and offer some help?"

The harried woman replied, "Anything, sir, anything!"

The child psychologist was called. "I want my boy to go home, but he won't leave," the mother explained.

The man thought a moment, then said, "I believe I can help." He approached the boy, who was about to get into a kiddie car, leaned over and whispered something in the youngster's ear. The kid looked startled, ran to his mother, grabbed her hand and said, "Come on, Mom, let's go."

In amazement she said, "Stay right here for a moment. I've got to talk to that man." "Sir," she asked, "what on earth did you say to my boy? I've been trying to get him to leave for an hour. I've begged, cajoled, bribed, without success. You come down, whisper a few words in his ear, and he's ready to leave. What on earth did you say to him?''

"Why, Madam, it's very simple," the child psychologist explained, "I just leaned over and said, 'Listen here, you little brat, if you don't get out of here, I'm going to set your britches on fire!' "

This homey anecdote illustrates a grave truth about our time. In our eagerness for freedom and spontaneity, we have forgotten that discipline is indispensable to proper development. We are suffering from an anemic, saccharin-pale concept of love, when, in fact, love is anything but an easy sentiment.

At the core of tough love is the awareness that there is no strength of character or achievement without discipline. Nothing worthwhile is ever achieved without struggle, pain and sacrifice. Everything we have of value is cradled in a discipline that hurts. And, despite our sophistication, we never seem to outgrow the need for such discipline. As someone wisely observed, "Every man is as lazy as he dares to be."

Tough love is hard for most of us. We're too insecure. Too immature. We want and need to be loved too much. Fortunately for us, God is neither insecure nor immature. Among many things, He is security with a capital "S." Maturity with a capital "M." While He wants our love and has gone to great lengths to gain it—look at Calvary—God is unwilling to pay too great a price for our love. Whenever necessary, whether we like it or not, He chastens us.

C. S. Lewis spoke with keen insight when he said, "God whispers to us in our pleasure, speaks to us in our conscience, but shouts to us in our pain. It is God's megaphone to rouse a deaf world."[1]

Now, it's important to distinguish between tough love

161

and the wrath of God. Whenever anyone meets Christ at Calvary, God's wrath toward that person, because of his sin, is dealt with once for all. No Christian shall ever be subjected to the wrath of God. But the disciplines of the heavenly Father toward us saved sinners are for purification, not condemnation.

The word "chasten" springs from two French words: *Castus,* meaning "pure," and *agere,* meaning "to drive." To chasten someone is to be driven by a desire to make that person pure. It is this driving concern which causes God to chasten us, His children.

Those New Testament references to severe and sudden acts of God in dealing with His children are not outbursts of His wrath. They are indications of His righteous indignation expressed in tough love. God cares deeply for the spiritual health and growth of His children. He will not stand idly by while we remain weak and ineffective when, through discipline, He can make us pure and strong.

The New Testament speaks of two forms of discipline: gentle discipline and severe discipline. The gentle way is that purging which follows a confession of sins. "If we confess our sins, He is faithful and righteous to forgive us our sins and to cleanse us [make us pure] from all unrighteousness" (I John 1:9). The severe way is through physical weakness and, in extreme cases, premature death. "For this reason many among you are weak and sick, and a number sleep [have died]" (I Corinthians 11:30).

The scripture is also clear that we need never be subjected to this second or severe way if we will hasten to employ the first or gentle way. If we face up to the fact of our sin, call it by its right name, confess and turn away from it, God will forgive us and impart to us the purity of Christ. That's tender love. It is spoken of in the first two verses of Hebrews 12 where, with great empathy for our struggle, we are told to lay aside every weight. To run with patience and endurance. To resist the ever-present temptation to quit before the race is over. And, to do so by faith in the bare word of God and the character of Christ who has run the race before us.

But, if we won't respond to tender love by voluntarily laying aside those things which encumber us, God loves us enough to exercise the tougher fiber of His love. God dares to discipline, and He does so just because He loves.

TOUGH LOVE

As our author will explain, training through discipline is never fun (12:11). There's a strong temptation to feel sorry for one's self. To develop a "Why me?" attitude. To wallow around in the slough of self-pity. So, he begins his discussion of tough love with this admonition: "For consider Him who has endured such hostility by sinners against Himself, so that you may not grow weary and lose heart" (12:3).

The best antidote for self-pity is to remember Jesus and what He went through. This will help you keep things in perspective. However heavy a burden you're having to bear, it is not nearly so sharp or serious as that which our Saviour bore. "He came to His own [home] and those who were His own did not receive Him" (John 1:11). Though innocent, He ". . . was numbered with the transgressors . . ." (Isaiah 53:12). He ". . . endured the cross, despising the shame . . ." (12:2), and sought no relief.

On the other hand, we who elect to follow Him often want instant answers to all our problems. We look for swift, easy escape from all tension, trial and tears. We want the power of His resurrection without the fellowship of His suffering. But that isn't possible. The Christian life was never meant to be a picnic. It's bound to be rough. It was rough for Jesus. It will be rough for you. The disciple is not above his Teacher (Matthew 10:24).

After all, the writer of Hebrews declares, the very fact God bothers to discipline you is evidence of His love. "And you have forgotten the exhortation which is addressed to you as sons, 'My son, do not regard lightly the discipline of the Lord, nor faint when you are reproved by Him; For those whom the Lord loves He disciplines, And He scourges every son whom He receives.' It is for discipline that you endure; God deals with you as with sons; for what son is there whom his father does not discipline? But if you are without discipline, of which all have become partakers, then you are illegitimate children and not sons" (12:5-8).

But this stirring statement is not God's final word on pain or suffering. As Charles R. Erdman says, "We must not conclude that God is the author of evil, nor that pain is always punishment, that suffering is a proof of sin." [2] To do so would be to reach very cruel and quite erroneous conclusions. Christ suffered and He was without sin. I suspect we should have to be God to get all the right answers regarding suffering. One thing is clear, however; God does not ordain everything He allows. But, if we will let Him, He will use what He allows to fulfill what He ordains.

God ordained that I should be a minister of the gospel. God did not ordain that my mother should die of cancer at the age of 56. However, God has used what He allowed—her premature death—to fulfill what He ordained: that I might be a more effective, caring, compassionate pastor. As a result of having witnessed the long, difficult death of my mother, I have been able to enter with great empathy into the agony and pain of those who lose their loved ones. God does not ordain everything He allows. But, if we will let Him, He will use what He allows to fulfill what He ordains.

All suffering is not a result or a proof of sin. But all suffering can be used by God for our profit if we take the right attitude toward it. God wants to operate through our personal situations and circumstances to train us for more effective service. He does so because we belong to Him. Hebrews 12:5-8 and other passages (Genesis 50:20; Romans 8:28) should reassure and fortify us. They indicate that disciplines of one sort or another are evidence of our sonship. We belong to God. He cares what happens to us.

To put it another way, discipline is the opposite of indifference. It is a mark of true caring. A precocious six-year-old grasped that truth. She and her sister were staying with us some years ago following the separation of her parents. To help them feel a part of our family, they were encouraged to call me Uncle John.

One day their mother explained the six-year-old was quite distressed because I hadn't given her any spankings. Actually, there had been no need to discipline her because she had been a model child. But she was anxious nonetheless and conveyed this to her mother, who passed it on to me. "Do you suppose Uncle John will spank me once in awhile, Mommy, just so I'll know he really cares?"

Love does not make discipline unnecessary. To the contrary, love and discipline are Siamese twins. If you are left without discipline, the writer of Hebrews says, you should really be concerned. A Christian's greatest problem is having no problem!

The other day I stopped by a business office in our town and ran into a young man whom I hadn't seen for months. I told him I'd missed him and asked how it was between him and God.

"Not good," he said. "But, oddly enough, it doesn't bother me. I've come to a kind of peace about it all."

As he spoke, a chill went down my spine. We are to be pitied most when we can sin and feel comfortable about it. It either means God has given up on us, or we were never His in the first place.

God doesn't discipline the devil's kids. He chastens His own. Discipline is God's method of training us for more effective service. Of preparing us for more strenuous tests to come. Of proving His love. When we see this, we will not only thank Him, we will worship Him with reverential awe (12:28). Discipline implies love on the part of the discipliner (12:6). Don't rebel against it. Or drop out under it. Accept it. Grow strong through it. God only chastens His own.

Our author also explains there is nothing cruel or capricious about God's discipline. Human parents sometimes goof in raising their kids. They do what they think is right and it turns out to be wrong. ". . . They disciplined us for a short time as seemed best to them . . ." (12:10a). On occasion they err in both method and purpose.

God never goofs, the writer of Hebrews says. He works in the right way for the right purpose. "He disciplines us for our good, that we may share His holiness" (12:10b). Though hard to endure, the end result makes God's discipline worthwhile. "All discipline for the moment seems not to be joyful, but sorrowful; yet to those who have been trained by it, afterwards it yields the peaceful fruit of righteousness" (12:11).

T. H. Robinson is correct in his observation that "no healthy person enjoys pain. It wouldn't be pain if he did. But a person may be induced to tolerate it, even welcome it, if he knows it will result to his advantage."[3]

For most of us, regular physical exercise is a bummer. It's boring and difficult. We hate it, though we persist in it, because it feels so good when we're done! The real reward comes, however, when those toughened muscles, lungs and heart are called upon to meet a sudden crisis and are equal to the challenge. Then the pain and boredom of discipline give way to the joy and satisfaction of achievement.

To pursue the illustration a bit further, when you get involved in a program of calisthenics and begin to work out regularly, the old tired cells within your body break down, die, and are sloughed off. But, if you properly nourish your body, those old dead cells are replaced by new, vital, stronger. larger, living cells. There must be a breakdown of the old before the new can come. It is this end result which makes the exercise program worthwhile.

So, too, with the disciplines of God. They are never fun when we're going through them. The good Lord doesn't want you to screw on a smile and run around shouting "Hallelujah, it hurts." But when, through discipline of one kind or another, you begin to enjoy the "peaceful fruit of righteousness" (12:11), then, though you can never say, "Hallelujah, it hurts," you can say, "Hallelujah, it helps!" You are able to join the Psalmist (119:67,71) in his bold affirmation:

> Before I was afflicted I went astray,
> But now I keep Thy word.
> It is good for me that I was afflicted,
> That I may learn Thy statutes.

No discipline is enjoyable while it is occurring, but afterwards there is "the peaceful fruit of righteousness." I love that phrase. It is so true to life. Oh, there is a kind of excitement and electricity about the early stages of the sinful life. But only for a season. Before long we literally become sick and tired of sinning. We are increasingly repelled and wearied by it all. As one young person said after he had experimented briefly with the drug scene, "It just wasn't worth the hassle!"

That can never be said about "the peaceful fruit of righteousness." It *is* worth the discipline involved to be able to look in the mirror and like what you see. To pillow your head at night knowing you are right with God, yourself and others. Feeling clean clear through is experiencing the peace that passes understanding (Philippians 4:7, KJV). And, though sin is slow to relinquish its hold on us, every taste of "the peaceful fruit of righteousness" awakens our desire for more, and strengthens our resolve to turn from sin toward God's way.

Having discussed God's willingness to resort to tough love when needed, our author returns to the firm but gentler appeal of tender love. "Strengthen the hands that are weak and the knees that are feeble" (12:12). Here he reverts to the language of the coliseum used earlier (12:1,2). We are to run with patience and perseverance, doing so for two reasons: one personal, the other corporate.

As we have already seen, some of those first-century Jesus Folk had run out of gas. They were so low spiritually they had to reach up to touch bottom. They were discouraged. About to toss in the towel. Their enthusiasm and interest was on the wane. Their commitment had grown thin. Those of more sturdy spiritual stock were instructed to hang tough for their own sake—to personally reach the goal—but also for the sake of their weaker, more weary fellows. We must do the same. "Strengthen the hands that are weak and the knees that are feeble" is a phrase to encourage flagging spirits. To deter potential dropouts.

But we are not only to run with patience and endurance. We must also lay aside every weight and be on guard against besetting sin. "... Make straight paths for your feet, so that the limb which is lame may not be put out of joint . . ." (12:13). Our calling is to persevere for our own sake and for the sake of others. We must walk carefully for the same dual purpose.

We are to be aware of our own peculiar areas of vulnerability and to shun those people, places and practices most likely to "beset us." Following the hand-eye severance principle (Matthew 5:29, 30), we must deal forthrightly with that to which we are most susceptible. We are to go to the root of our problem. Cut it off. Dig it out. For our own sake and for the sake of others.

Our author's reference to "... the limb which is lame . . ." (12:13) is another invitation to think Hebrew. He is drawing a word picture of those faltering between Jesus and Jesus-plus. Unless these limping Christians find spiritual healing they may soon be so disabled as to drop out of the race permanently, with serious loss of present blessing and future reward. "See to it that no one comes short [fails] . . ." (12:15). With tough love, help each other to hang tough. "Pursue after peace with all men, and after the sanctification without which no man will see the Lord" (12:14).

Many have been bothered by this last statement, as stated in the Authorized Version: "Follow peace with all men, and holiness, without which no man shall see the Lord." But its true meaning becomes clear when we realize that the same word translated "holiness" here is translated "sanctify" elsewhere in the book of Hebrews. To be sanctified is "to be put to the proper use." That becomes possible when, by faith, you acknowledge God was in Christ and Christ is in you.

As that marvelous truth settles in, you know who you are and what you are. Knowing those two things, you also know how you are to be used. You know your talent, training, time and treasure are not to be used exclusively, or even primarily, for your own personal profit, but for God's purposes. When you know how you are to be used, your priorities begin to change. Your values clarify. Your witness takes on the sound of certainty. Your life bears the mark of eternity.

You are being to the world what Christ would be if He were here Himself. And that's holiness! Holiness of the highest order. Of a most practical kind. The holiness which enables you to see God more clearly, but, better yet, enables others to see God more clearly in you!

In and through all this, our author holds before us the grim specter of lost blessing and reward. Look after each other so no one fails to enjoy God's best blessings (12:15a). Support, help and, if necessary, correct each other to avoid the tragic cost of bitterness and flippancy (12:15b).

Bitterness is always wrong. Always. Without exception. No matter how justified. Bitterness is a contagious disease which, in its more virulent forms, can be spiritually fatal. The same must be said for its viral twin, flippancy. It actually ruined Esau. This man who came to stand for things earthy and sensual looked upon his birthright with such flippant disdain that he sold it for a single meal (Genesis 25:28-34).

That birthright was very important. It had to do with God's promise to Abraham and the blessing his seed had been blessed to be. Esau was part of Abraham's seed. When he treated this promise of God lightly, he was saying, in effect, what God offers to do in, to, for and through us merits little more than a shrug. This flippancy deprived Esau forever from blessing on earth and reward in heaven. (The reference to "no immoral or godless person like Esau" (12:16) is not to physical adultery, but to spiritual whoredom—the worshiping of other gods than Jehovah.)

Later, Esau had some second thoughts. He tried to gain back the paternal blessing (Genesis 27:1-38), but it was impossible. ". . . He found no place for repentance . . ." (12:17). This does not mean Esau was barred forever from the forgiveness of God. It simply means that there are certain choices which cannot be undone. Certain consequences even God cannot—will not—change.

William Barclay gives a simple, but pointed, illustration. If a boy loses his purity or a girl her virginity, nothing can ever bring it back. Nothing can change the physical fact. The choice was made. The consequence stands. God can and will forgive. And, in His eyes, moral innocence will be restored. But God Himself cannot turn back the clock, unmake the choice and undo the consequence. Something has happened which can never be undone.[4]

Esau ". . . found no place for repentance . . ." (12:17). Isaac, his father, could not restore the blessing taken from one son and given to another. The birthright was lost. ". . . though he sought for it with tears" (12:17). But notice: Esau did not lose his *sonship*. That's important. He lost his *birthright*. He forfeited the opportunity to be a blessing and receive a blessing through the proper exercise of that birthright. *But Esau was still his father's boy.*

This passage does not teach a child of God can be saved and then lost. What it does solemnly warn against is the danger of repeating Esau's mistake. Of taking a flippant attitude toward our spiritual birthright as Jesus persons.

Of looking casually and carelessly upon God's promise to bless us in order that we might be a blessing, thus suffering the subsequent loss of time, opportunity and reward which can never be retrieved.

Therefore, our author urges, use all the resources available in resisting the ever-present temptation to sell God and yourself short. Victory will come, he says, only when you make full and proper use of your Christian birthright. You have not been called to Mount Sinai, the place of gloom. ". . . You have come to Mount Zion"(12:22a), the place of grace. "And to the city of the living God, the heavenly Jerusalem" (12:22b), that spiritual kingdom within each believer which Jesus characterized as the Kingdom of God.

"And to myriads of angels" (12:22c), those ministering spirits who, at God's direction, are everlastingly busy bringing aid and comfort to us as we run our race. Yes, angels are part of our spiritual inheritance. And "to the general assembly and church of the first-born who are enrolled in heaven" (12:23a), that amazing fellowship called the church. A fellowship which conquers the differences dividing us, the difficulties facing us, the despair assailing us.

Thank God, the church is part of our resource and birthright. "And to God, the judge of all" (12:23b), whose every godly asset and attribute is at the disposal of those who belong to Him. "And to the spirits of righteous men made perfect" (12:23c), another reference to that "great . . . cloud of witnesses" who cheer us on and remind us it can be done because they did it.

"And to Jesus, the mediator of a new covenant" (12:24a), a new arrangement for living whereby everything God asks of us He gives to us in the person of Jesus. "And to the sprinkled blood, which speaks better than the blood of Abel" (12:24b). The blood of Abel cried out for vengeance and justly so (Genesis 4:10), but the blood of Jesus cries out for forgiveness and mercy (Luke 23:34).

All this is included in your spiritual birthright. It is yours, to help you run with patience, and resist the temptation to drop out. Reckon on all your resources. God is eager and able to aid you if you'll only ask Him.

A father watched his young son struggle to move a huge boulder which was in his way. The boy tugged and pulled, straining every muscle without success. Finally, the father walked over and said, "Son, why don't you use all your resources?"

In frustration the boy barked back, "Dad, how can you say that when I'm straining every muscle to budge this boulder? I am using all my resources!"

"No, you aren't," his father replied quietly. "You haven't asked me to help."

WARNING AND HOPE

The four final verses of chapter 12 contain a word of hope springing from tough love. The dominant note is one of assurance. The time will come when, through a single decisive act in history, God, who brought the material universe into being, will bring it to an end (12:26). But Jesus Folk can rejoice and give thanks. We belong to a spiritual realm which cannot be shaken (12:27,28). This is not to say Christians will escape the final shaking. But it is a promise we shall come through unscathed. We will survive. Why? Because, as we read in Romans 8:35-39, the one thing nothing can destroy is the relationship between ourselves and God.

Therefore, we should show our gratitude by our service offered with reverence and awe. "For our God is a consuming fire" (12:29). What a reason to rejoice! To give thanks and worship God with reverence and awe. We belong to a God who will resort to tough love when necessary. Who cares so deeply about us He cannot and will not stand idly by as we are made weak and ineffective by unpurged evil. So He subjects us to the refining fire.

Someone has wisely noted: Fire will destroy what it cannot purify, and purify what it cannot destroy. The one thing which cannot be destroyed is the relationship between ourselves and God. Because our heavenly Father wants that relationship to be without spot and blemish, He submits it to the purifying fire of His love and light.

That fire is our hope. It means, my fellow sinner-saint, you will never come to God with an act of confession and repentance and turn away unforgiven. Nor will you turn away without having been made clean clear through by the consuming fire which purifies what it cannot destroy. God dares to discipline. He loves with a tough love. A love which insists upon destroying everything without and within which keeps us from being like Jesus, who one day will ". . . present [us] faultless [made pure by the consuming fire] before the presence of his glory with exceeding joy (Jude 1:24, KJV). Truly it begs to be said—hallelujah!

10

In Conclusion, Brethren

Hebrews 13

LET love of the brethren continue. ²Do not neglect to show hospitality to strangers, for by this some have entertained angels without knowing it. ³Remember the prisoners, as though in prison with them, and those who are ill-treated, since you yourselves also are in the body. ⁴Let marriage be held in honor among all, and let the marriage bed be undefiled; for fornicators and adulterers God will judge. ⁵Let your way of life be free from the love of money, being content with what you have; for He Himself has said, "I will never desert you, nor will I ever forsake you," ⁶so that we confidently say,

"The Lord is my helper, I will not be afraid.
What shall man do to me?"

⁷Remember those who led you, who spoke the word of God to you; and considering the outcome of their way of life, imitate their faith. ⁸Jesus Christ is the same yesterday and today, yes and forever. ⁹Do not be carried away by varied and strange teachings; for it is good for the heart to be strengthened by grace, not by foods, through which those who were thus occupied were not benefited. ¹⁰We have an altar, from which those who serve the tabernacle have no right to eat.

[11]*For the bodies of those animals whose blood is brought into the holy place by the high priest as an offering for sin, are burned outside the camp.* [12]*Therefore Jesus also, that He might sanctify the people through His own blood, suffered outside the gate.* [13]*Hence, let us go out to Him outside the camp, bearing His reproach.* [14]*For here we do not have a lasting city, but we are seeking the city which is to come.* [15]*Through Him then let us continually offer up a sacrifice of praise to God, that is, the fruit of lips that give thanks to His name.* [16]*And do not neglect doing good and sharing; for with such sacrifices God is pleased.*

[17]*Obey your leaders, and submit to them; for they keep watch over your souls, as those who will give an account. Let them do this with joy and not with grief, for this would be unprofitable for you.* [18]*Pray for us, for we are sure that we have a good conscience, desiring to conduct ourselves honorably in all things.* [19]*And I urge you all the more to do this, that I may be restored to you the sooner.*

[20]*Now the God of peace, who brought up from the dead the great Shepherd of the sheep through the blood of the eternal covenant, even Jesus our Lord,* [21]*equip you in every good thing to do His will, working in us that which is pleasing in His sight, through Jesus Christ, to whom be the glory forever and ever. Amen.*

[22]*But I urge you, brethren, bear with this word of exhortation, for I have written to you briefly.* [23]*Take notice that our brother Timothy has been released, with whom, if he comes soon, I shall see you.* [24]*Greet all of your leaders and all the saints. Those from Italy greet you.*

[25]*Grace be with you all.*

Who Jesus is and what Jesus did have been two of three major strands threading throughout the book of Hebrews. The third—what this means in terms of life for today and hope for tomorrow—has intertwined the other two so tightly at times it has been difficult for us to tell them apart. But, as our author draws his letter to a close, he spotlights this third emphasis—focusing our attention on certain practical applications of authentic Christianity, particularly those qualities we Jesus people must project in our working relationships with each other and in our witness to the world.

A list of these virtues might read as follows: *empathy, hospitality, sympathy, purity, simplicity, loyalty, fidelity, charity* and *true piety.* Capping them off is a blessed doxology followed by a grand amen. On the twin notes of peace and praise, the book of Hebrews ends.

EMPATHY

The first of these vital virtues we should point toward as Christians is empathy. "Let love of the brethren continue" (13:1). What our author commends here is more than a warm, tender feeling of affection. It is love in long trousers. Mature. Levelheaded. Dependable. A core-deep tie which will bind Christians together, come what may.

Taken in the context in which it is set, brotherly love is an awareness of and sensitivity to the inner struggle through which our fellow saved sinners may be going.

Suspiciousness was a grave temptation for those early Hebrew converts. It was easy for them to be constantly evaluating the orthodoxy of their fellows because reversion to a religion of Jesus-plus was a constant threat. Brotherly love is that which can help them support each other, while avoiding the lurking impulse to become heresy hunters when right believing was so important to their spiritual survival.

For Jesus persons today it means that and more. As we have seen, the Christian life is not easy. To have empathy for one another is to climb into the other guy's skin and look back at life through his eyes, fears, doubts and tears, being so sensitized by what we see we can only nestle our fellow Christian in supportive, redemptive, liberating love and understanding.

This is what each of you needs and deserves from the other, the writer of Hebrews says. Don't judge or be forever suspicious of each other. Don't constantly test the other person's theological blood-type. Cling to God in Christ and hang loose on everything else. Let sensitized, empathetic, brotherly love continue.

HOSPITALITY

"Do not neglect to show hospitality to strangers, for by this some have entertained angels without knowing it" (13:2). Our author employs an intensely interesting Greek word in writing about "hospitality to strangers." I can find only one other place in the New Testament where this particular Greek word is used. Every other Biblical mention of "strangers" uses Greek words having to do with foreigners. Aliens. Those who are completely unknown to us. Both of these New Testament references (13:2 and Romans 12:13) are to fellow Jesus Folk. The strangers our author mentions here are strangers who should not be strangers! Members of the Christian brotherhood we should know better and love more than we do.

To those first-century Christians, where each local church fellowship was so small it was possible to be on a first-name basis with everyone, this "hospitality to strangers" probably meant being open and friendly to itinerant preachers who might be passing through town. Or to fleeing refugees who had been driven from their homes because of their Christian commitment.

In our time, I think it means something quite different. We are to be kind to Christian guests, of course. But the primary application of this principle for us today is the extending of hospitality or plain, old-fashioned Christian kindness to the "stranger" who sits next to us in the pew. The person we meet in church every Sunday, but only nod to. The isolated soul who is a member of the same Sunday School class. Who attends the same woman's circle. Who participates in the same Bible study group. Who shares in the same youth activity, yet, whom we don't really know or even care about.

In California, where I live, this may be a carry-over of the six-foot fence philosophy which separates us from our neighbors, their hurts and their needs. In other parts of our country and world, different methods are used to isolate one's self from the pain and problems of others. When these isolation methods creep into the church, as they often do, and become standard practice—as in many cases they have—we need to be jerked up short by this stern admonition, "Do not neglect to show hospitality to strangers, for by this some have entertained angels without knowing it" (13:2).

How true that is! Often we set out to provide some small ministry to another, only to wind up being ministered to ourselves. We sometimes entertain an "angel"—a ministering spirit—and discover we have been more blessed than we were a blessing. I recall a hospital call I made on a dear saint. Her name was Arnola Hershey. Though very old, she was as bright as a silver dollar. We visited about the many things of interest to her. Then, taking her hand, I prayed. For her son and daughter. Her grandchildren. Her church. The needs of others which were always high on her list of loving concern. I said, "Amen" and drew my hand away.

She reached out, pulled it back, and without a pause began praying for *me*. "And God, bless Dr. John, too. Bless his wife. His children. His work for our church. And never let him down in any important way." For several minutes she held me up before the Lord.

Now I've made thousands of hospital calls and prayed for hundreds of sick people. But this was the first time a patient ever prayed for me! I couldn't hold back the tears. As I left Arnola's room that day, I knew I had entertained an angel unaware.

SYMPATHY

"Remember the prisoners, as though in prison with them, and those who are ill-treated, since you yourselves also are in the body" (13:3). The characteristic here is sympathy, but it is sympathy of a very special kind. Not the clinically sterile, legislated variety so common today. That kind of pitiful pity demeans and dehumanizes people. Instead of a patronizing, professionalized sympathy, we are to express the compassion Christ expressed by doing as Jesus did. We are to take our place alongside those in need as if we were one of them. Remembering that, but for the grace of God, the tables might well be turned. It might be we rather than they in need of kindness and caring.

PURITY

The fourth virtue our author says must spring from a vital life-changing relationship with Jesus is personal purity. "Let marriage be held in honor among all, and let the marriage bed be undefiled; for fornicators and adulterers God will judge" (13:4). According to my friends close to the Jesus movement, particularly as it relates to college and career young people, sex is one of the last areas they are willing to put under the Lordship of Jesus.

In that regard, these Jesus kids are not terribly different from some segments of the first-century church. A proper use of the sex energy has been a challenge to many, if not most, Christians. Failure in this area has often been devastating to the spiritually newborn.

Dr. Earl Wilson, one of our Project Winsome lay leaders, holds a Ph.D. in clinical psychology and trains doctoral candidates in that specialty at the University of Nebraska. One night Earl and I were talking about the various crisis points for Christians. He indicated they had learned, on campus at least, the major danger point was immediately after a new Christian's first moral failure, which was usually of a sexual nature. Unless these young people had been told in advance that being a Christian did not make them immune to evil, that they would still be tempted and on occasion might fall, they were so devastated by this failure they were ready to junk the Christian life on the premise, "It didn't work."

"But," said Dr. Wilson, "if we can be there after that first big failure with the message of recurring repentance and forgiveness for recurring sin following conversion, they usually pick themselves up and go on from victory to victory, handling the various and occasional other defeats as a Christian should."

Recent converts are not the only ones who have trouble

in the area of sex. Some who become Christians before they could even spell S-E-X have had similar struggles in later years. In every instance, God has resorted to discipline. The question is, which form of discipline do we force Him to use? The gentle form springing from a burning conscience which must be cleansed through confession, repentance and forgiveness? Or the severe kind resulting in emotional, physical and spiritual illness of one sort or another?

Let it be said again: God dares to discipline. He cares deeply about the well-being of His own. He knows the importance of stable Christian homes and will do everything He can to protect them. Therefore, the writer of Hebrews says, Let personal purity be the hallmark of all your relationships. "Let marriage be held in honor among all, and let the marriage bed be undefiled . . ." (13:4).

SIMPLICITY

Next, strive for simplicity in your life-style. "Let your way of life be free from the love of money, being content with what you have; for He Himself has said, 'I will never desert you, nor will I forsake you' " (13:5). Hence we can confidently say, " 'The Lord is my helper, I will not be afraid. What shall man do to me?' " (13:6).

These verses are open to easy misinterpretation leading to the quite erroneous conclusion that money is evil and wealth is anti-Christian. Neither is true. The teaching here is not that we should avoid money, but the love of money. We are to steer clear of letting gold be our god. There is a vast difference between love of money and a talent for making money. The first is hell-born. The second is God-given and, if used for His glory and mankind's good, can be an enormous blessing.

Simplicity in the Christian's life-style is, of course, a highly relative thing. Most Americans enjoy a standard of living exceeding that of kings a few hundred years ago. It seems to me, therefore, a safe guideline in this area for Christians is whether we own our possessions or they own us. Whether we are the user or the used. If the latter is true, we are in trouble. We are vulnerable to what men can do to us. But if we can say, "The Lord is my helper," we will be able to take whatever comes with Christian grace, knowing God works in everything, wealth as well as poverty, for good to those who love Him (Romans 8:28).

LOYALTY

Loyalty is another quality commended to Jesus people. "Remember those who led you, who spoke the word of God to you; and considering the outcome of their way of life, imitate their faith" (13:7). "Obey your leaders, and submit to them; for they keep watch over your souls, as those who will give an account. Let them do this with joy and not with grief, for this would be unprofitable for you" (13:17).

In a sentence, be like my friend, Mel Anderson. Now retired, Mel made a commitment to Jesus as a young man, that he would try, with God's help, to be the kind of layman who would cause his pastor's heart to rejoice. Whose name would precipitate feelings of gladness and gratitude, rather than grim regret at having to deal with such a difficult, negative person.

I can say from seven years of delightful experience as one of those privileged to be his pastor, Mel Anderson reached his objective. He was a pastor's layman in the highest sense of that term. I was able to watch over his soul with joy, not with grief (13:17b). Be that kind of

Christian, the writer of Hebrews says. Be a person who always gives more than he takes.

In his letter to the church at Philippi, Paul has a lovely sentence all Jesus Folk might well wish was written to them. "I thank my God in all my remembrance of you" (Philippians 1:3). What a beautiful thought! But even better, what a beautiful way to be thought of! It's just that kind of memory I want your leaders to have of you, the writer of Hebrews says. I want them to be able to say, "I thank my God in all my remembrance of you."

FIDELITY

The seventh of these spotlighted virtues is doctrinal fidelity. While our author gives considerable space to this (verses 8-15), we shan't, because it is a recapitulation of everything we have already covered in great detail: the unrivaled supremacy and unchanging sufficiency of Jesus who is the same today as He was yesterday, and as He shall be tomorrow (13:8). He identified Himself with us in our disgrace "outside the gate" (13:12). Therefore, we should be willing to bear any abuse for His sake (13:13), remembering it is no virtue to conform to this world when our true citizenship is in heaven (13:14).

CHARITY

Moving on, we discover charity to be a virtue of great value for sinner-saints. "And do not neglect doing good and sharing; for with such sacrifices God is pleased" (13:16). How reminiscent of the words of our Lord: " 'Truly I say to you, to the extent that you did it to one of these brothers of Mine, even the least of them, you did it to Me' " (Matthew 25:40).

In Barre, Vermont, there is a famous granite quarry

called "The Rock of Ages." It is tremendous. Over 200 feet deep, I'm told. One day a friend of mine, Dr. Clarence Cranford, visited the quarry.

As the superintendent pointed out the vastness of this excavation, he made an interesting comment. "We've gone as deep as we can without going wider."

"What do you mean?" Dr. Cranford inquired.

"Just that," the man explained. "Even though the walls of the quarry are solid granite, the pressure from the surrounding earth is so great that if we go deeper without going wider, we could have a cave-in. We've gone as deep as we can without going wider."

Many of us Jesus Folk say, "Oh, God, deepen my Christian life!" Could God be saying, "Oh, child of Mine, widen your Christian life! You can't go deeper till you go wider. Reach out to those about you. Share what I have given you in such abundance, both materially and spiritually. In the process of going wider, you will go deeper. You will find your own relationship with Me growing stronger and sweeter."

PIETY

The last of these qualities elevated in our thinking is piety. Not "pietism"—a situation in which the means often become an end in themselves—but piety. That is, true spirituality defined as prayer, a clear conscience, an honest life (13:18). "I urge you all the more to do this" (13:19a).

Volumes could be written on the next two verses. They contain one of the most gracious of all benedictions. One of the most inspiring of all doxologies. "Now the God of peace, who brought up from the dead the great Shepherd of the sheep through the blood of the eternal covenant, even Jesus our Lord, equip you in every good thing to do

His will, working in us that which is pleasing in His sight, through Jesus Christ, to whom be the glory forever and ever. Amen'' (13:20,21).   Our God is the God of peace. Our God is the God of life. Our God is the God who both shows us His will and equips us to do it through Jesus. Jesus, the Great Shepherd, who not only guides God's flock, but also gave Himself for our eternal safekeeping through a new relationship signed and sealed in His blood. On the twin notes of peace and praise the book of Hebrews ends.[1]

The persistent theme throughout our study has been *Jesus*. Who He is. What He did. All He means in terms of life for today and hope for tomorrow. A book such as this on a theme such as that cannot properly end without one last invitation to let Jesus Christ be Saviour and Lord. I extend it through the pen of Billy Rose.

Years ago in one of his newspaper columns, Mr. Rose told the story of an Albany surgeon who was awakened at 2:30 one morning by a call from a fellow physician at the hospital in Glenn Falls, New York, some sixty miles away. A small boy was critical. Without immediate surgery, the child would die. He was the only qualified surgeon within driving distance. They could keep the boy alive for up to an hour and a half. Would the surgeon come? Of course!

He quickly dressed, backed his car out, drove down the residential streets to the main intersection of downtown Albany. While waiting for a red light to change, the door opposite him opened and a man jumped in. The doctor noted the intruder wore a dirty brown cap pulled low over his eyes, a brown suede jacket, a sport shirt open at the throat and a pair of grey slacks. In his hand was a gun.

"Drive on," he said. The doctor did as he was told. Each time he tried to engage the man in conversation, the reply was, "Shut up and keep driving." When they were well outside the city, the man said, "Pull over and stop." The doctor obeyed. "Get out," the man ordered.

Risking his life the physician pleaded, "I'm a surgeon on an emergency mission. A patient will die unless I am there within a very short time."

"I don't care about that," the man retorted, "get out!" He forced the doctor out of the car and drove off into the night.

The surgeon hurried to a nearby farmhouse, awakened the family and, using their telephone, called a cab company in Albany. As quickly as possible, the taxi transported him to Glenn Falls. By the time he arrived two hours had elapsed. The surgeon dashed up the steps to the hospital and through the doors, where he was greeted by the physician who had called him. "It's too late. The boy just died."

Crestfallen, the surgeon explained the delay. His friend understood. They could talk about it later over coffee. "But right now, come into the waiting room. The boy's father is here. It will comfort him to know you tried so hard to get here."

The doctor entered the waiting room. There sat the father, head in hands, his shoulders shaking convulsively with grief. On the chair beside him lay a dirty brown hat. He wore a brown suede jacket, a sport shirt open at the throat and a pair of grey slacks. Here was the father who had pushed out of the car the only man on earth who could have saved the life of his son.

The application is clear. Do not push out of your life the only One who can complete it. Do not reject Jesus! Or, if you have already received Him, do not neglect Jesus. He is the same yesterday, today and forever. To paraphrase another, as far as your own life and time are concerned, yesterday is already a dream and tomorrow is just a vision. But, every today lived with Jesus will make every yesterday a dream of happiness and every tomorrow a vision of hope!

Notes

1. OUR HOPE: Jesus Helps Us Grow

1. From Morgan Park Baptist Church bulletin, "Advance," Chicago (1971). Ian Chapman is the pastor.
2. F. F. Bruce, *The Epistle to the Hebrews* (Grand Rapids, MI: Wm. B. Eerdmans Publishing Co., 1964), p. 127.
3. Ruth Harms Calkins, *Tell Me Again, Lord, I Forget!* (Elgin, IL: David C. Cook Publishing Company)

2. OUR HOPE: Jesus Jams Open the Door

1. M. R. DeHaan, *Hebrews* (Grand Rapids, MI: Zondervan Publishing House, 1959), p. 111.
2. A. John Nastari, *Questions Christ Asked* (Lake Oswego, OR: A. John Nastari, 2890 SW Dellwood Drive, Lake Oswego, OR 97034), p. 64.

3. OUR HOPE: Jesus—a Priest Like Mel Who?

1. Nastari, *Questions Christ Asked,* p. 41.
2. Harry A. Ironside, *Studies in the Epistle to the Hebrews* (New York: Loizeaux Brothers, 1932) p. 85.
3. Nancy Spiegelberg (Minneapolis, MN: *Decision* Magazine, 1971).

4. OUR HOPE: Jesus Completes a New Contract

1. William Barclay, *Epistle to the Hebrews* (New York and Nashville: Abingdon Press, 1965), p. 76.
2. Beverly Caviness (Minneapolis, MN: *Decision* Magazine).

5. OUR HOPE: Jesus Is All You Need

1. Barclay, *Epistle to the Hebrews,* p. 47.
2. Louis T. Talbot, *Christ in the Tabernacle* (Wheaton, IL: Van Kampen Press, 1942).

6. OUR HOPE: Jesus Is What's Happening

1. A. W. Tozer, "The Editorial Voice" (*The Alliance Witness,* 1962)

7. HIS SECOND COMING: Your Joy or Judgment

1. Theodore H. Robinson, *The Epistle to the Hebrews,* (London: Hodder and Stoughton, 1933), p. 144.
2. From "Sorrows of God" by G. A. Studert-Kennedy, quoted in *Pulpit Digest.* February, 1956.

8. HOW TO Hang Tough in a Hostile World

9. God Dares to Discipline

1. C. S. Lewis, *The Problem of Pain* (New York: The MacMillan Company, 1944), p. 81.
2. Charles R. Erdman, *The Epistle to the Hebrews* (Philadelphia, PA: Westminster Press, 1934), p. 132.
3. Robinson, *Epistle to the Hebrews,* p. 184.
4. Barclay, *Letter to the Hebrews,* p. 210.

10. In Conclusion, Brethren . . .

1. Barclay, The Letter to the Hebrews, p. 299ff.

Bibliography

Barclay, William and F. F. Bruce, editors, *Epistle to the Hebrews* (Lutterworth Press, London and Abingdon Press, New York and Nashville, jointly, 1965)

Barclay, William, *Letter to the Hebrews, The,* (The Saint Andrew Press, Edinburgh, 1955)

Baxter, J. Sidlow, *Explore the Book* (Sword of the Lord Publishers, Wheaton, IL; also Marshall, Morgan & Scott, Ltd., 33 Ludgate Hill, E.C.4, 1955)

Briston, Lyle O. *Hebrews, A Commentary* (The Judson Press, Valley Forge, PA, 1967

Bruce, F. F., *Epistle to the Hebrews, The* The New International Commentary on the New Testament (Wm. B. Eerdmans Publishing Co., Grand Rapids, MI, 1964)

DeHaan, *Hebrews* (Zondervan Publishing House, Grand Rapids, MI, 1959)

Erdman, Charles R., *Epistle to the Hebrews, The* (The Westminster Press, 1966)

Hewitt, Thomas, *Hebrews* (The Tyndale Press, 39 Bedford Square, W.C.1, London, 1960)

Ironside, H. A., *Studies in the Epistle to the Hebrews* (The American Bible Conference Association, Philadelphia, PA, 1932)

Lewis, C. S., *Problem of Pain, The* (The MacMillan Company, New York, 1944)

Manson, William, *Epistle to the Hebrews,* The (Hodder and Stoughton, St. Paul's House, Warwick Lane, London, E.C.4, 1951)

Meyer, F. B., *Meet for the Master's Use* (The Bible Institute Colportage Association, 843-845 North Wells Street, Chicago, IL 1898)

Morgan, G. Campbell, *Triumphs of Faith, The* (Fleming H. Revell Co., London and Edinburgh, 1945)

Morris, Leon, I Timothy—James, Scripture Union Bible Study Books (Wm. B. Eerdmans Publishing Company, Grand Rapids, MI, 1969

Nastari, A. John, *Questions Christ Asked* (2890 S.W. Dellwood Drive, Lake Oswego, OR 97034)

Robinson, Theodore H., *Epistle to the Hebrews,* The (Hodder and Stoughton, St. Paul's House, Warwick Lane, London, E.C.4, 1933)

Saxe, Grace, arranged by, *Studies In Hebrews* (Moody Press, Chicago, IL)

Talbot, Louis T., *Christ in the Tabernacle* (Van Kampen Press, Wheaton, IL, 1942)

Taylor, Charles Forbes, *Everlasting Salvation,* (Fleming H. Revell Co., 158 Fifth Avenue, New York, 1925)

To the Reader

If you have enjoyed *Hang Tough in a Hostile World* but have not yet read Dr. Lavender's fascinating study of the first half of Hebrews, *Hey! There's Hope!* you will want to secure a copy from your local bookstore or from Accent Books, PO Box 15337, Denver, Colorado 80215.